The Power in Pretend

Other Redleaf Press books by Mike Huber

Embracing Rough-and-Tumble Play: Teaching with the Body in Mind

Inclusion Includes Us: Building Bridges and Removing Barriers to Include All Children and Adults in Early Childhood Classrooms

Children's picture books by Mike Huber

All in One Day

The Amazing Erik

Bree Finds a Friend

Evette's Invitation

Mama's Gloves

Rita and the Firefighters

The Power in Pretend

Supporting Children's Power, Identity, and Agency

Mike Huber

Redleaf Press®
www.redleafpress.org
800-423-8309

Published by Redleaf Press
10 Yorkton Court
St. Paul, MN 55117
www.redleafpress.org

First edition 2025
Cover design by Jesse Hughes
Cover photographs from stock.adobe.com
Interior design by Becky Daum
Typeset in Adobe Garamond Pro
Printed in the United States of America
32 31 30 29 28 27 26 25 1 2 3 4 5 6 7 8

Library of Congress Cataloging-in-Publication Data

Names: Huber, Mike (Early childhood educator), author.
Title: The power in pretend : supporting children's power, identity, and
   agency / by Mike Huber.
Description: First edition. | St. Paul, MN : Redleaf Press, 2025. |
   Includes bibliographical references and index. | Summary: "Ranging from
   princess play to gun play, The Power in Pretend questions and sheds
   light on the ways children play with ideas of power. The book gives
   practical strategies for adults in early childhood settings to support
   this sense of power in pretend play and in real ways"— Provided by
   publisher.
Identifiers: LCCN 2024057642 (print) | LCCN 2024057643 (ebook) | ISBN
   9781605548487 (paperback) | ISBN 9781605548494 (ebook)
Subjects: LCSH: Play--Psychological aspects. | Control (Psychology) in
   children. | Imagination in children.
Classification: LCC BF717 .H83 2025 (print) | LCC BF717 (ebook) | DDC
   155.4/18--dc23/eng/20250215
LC record available at https://lccn.loc.gov/2024057642
LC ebook record available at https://lccn.loc.gov/2024057643

Printed on acid-free paper

For Richard Hess, my high school
drama club teacher,
who showed us the power
in pretend.

Contents

Acknowledgments

The ideas in this book have been dancing in my head for more than ten years. Like most ideas, my understanding of pretend play was simplistic in the beginning. The evolution from bumper-sticker thinking to a book involved contributions from so many people. Some people added to my ideas through intentional conversation or study while just as many contributed inadvertently with a tossed-off comment.

My thoughts around superhero and gun play first evolved through conversations with Becky Klay, Kristen Wheeler-Highland, Joey Schoen, Tom Bedard, and Ross Thompson. I started presenting workshops on the topic and my conversations moved beyond Minnesota, leading to panel discussions and hallway conversations with Josh Thomspon, Tim Kinard, and Lisa Murphy. I wouldn't have written this book without their knowledge and insight.

I also want to thank those who in small ways sparked my continued interest in the topic. A chance encounter with Diane Levin encouraged me to take my ideas on consent and gun play further. Another chance encounter with Sara Gilliam led to my continuing relationship with *Exchange* magazine, where I started to put down some of these ideas. Meanwhile, conversations on identity development that I had with Dan Hodgins, Remus Huber, Twisted Trans Sister, and so many others made me see how I was missing the big picture by only focusing on superhero and gun play and ignoring other types of pretend. That's when this book took shape.

As I worked on the book, I relied on many of my fellow early childhood nerds: Heather Bernt-Santy, Carol Garboden Murray, Kisa Marx, Kylie Cooper, and Annie Berres. I gained insight from Sonia Funkenbusch and Leya Charles precisely because they are not in the early childhood field. Last, this book would not exist without my editor, Melissa York. This book moves in many directions and Melissa kept me from veering too far off the path.

I want to thank everyone not just for their contributions to this book but also for the future conversations I know we will have.

Introduction

"Shhh, I'm working." Not-quite-three-year-old Maggie picks up a book from her mom's nightstand, flips it sideways, opens it, and starts clicking her fingers on her "laptop." She grabs a rolled-up sock to use as her mouse and is now "the Boss." She says to her mom, "You have to work too."

Mom smiles and picks up another book and imitates her Boss. Mom knows her role. "When do you need the rep—"

"Shhh! I'm on a call." The Boss looks at her screen and tells it, "Sorry, I was interrupted. We're having a meeting." Mom can't help laughing at what she must sound like to her daughter. But she is soon admonished, "You're not doing good work. You're fired."

Anyone who has spent even a little bit of time with a toddler or preschooler has probably experienced some version of this story. The child might be a lion, a superhero, a mom, or—like Maggie—even mom's boss, surely the most powerful person many children could imagine. In some ways, I think imagination is the root of power for all of us.

And that is what this book is about, imagination and power. I was originally asked to write a book about gun play, but I was hesitant. In fact, I was ready to turn it down. Then I went to opening night of the movie *Barbie* and was struck by how empowered so many people felt watching a story about a doll from their childhoods. This doll had the power to be anything: a doctor, a lawyer, a mermaid, and even the president. Meanwhile, there was a plethora of media coverage that was surprised that a movie about something as silly as a doll could be a blockbuster.

That's when I realized what was missing in writing only about gun play. There was an artificial binary underlying most attitudes about gun play. Boys are much more likely to engage in gun play, which is often considered scary. At the same time, girls are more likely to play with Barbie and other dolls, which is often considered silly. But both types of play get to the core of what drives most children: imagination and a sense of power.

I have reflected on children's strong inclination to take on roles of power in their pretend play over my thirty years of working with young children. Adults' fear regarding gun play has been relatively consistent during that time. I have continued reading articles and books, having conversations with others in the field, and trying different strategies with the children in my care, leading me to three main takeaways. The first is that you cannot fully understand what the children experience by simply watching from the outside. The second is that "othering" gun play as separate from other types of children's play makes it more difficult to understand and can, in fact, pathologize this type of play. And, finally, the third is that gun play is just one form of exploring power.

Understanding from the Outside

Play by its very nature is immersive; the occupation itself (see sidebar) is more important than any outcome. Children play for the purpose of playing. When I watched gun play or superhero play from the outside, I only saw it as mirroring real-life tragedy playing out in wider society. But I was watching it from my adult perspective. As philosopher Maurice Merleau-Ponty ([1945] 2002, 429) put it, I was experiencing this play "from a certain point of view." Being in the classroom during this play meant that I was connected. Or to quote Merleau-Ponty, "I am not the spectator, I am involved" (354). In other words, I was not going to understand the play only using my own point of view as if it were truth itself. I had to immerse myself in the play. That meant simply watching at first, silently trying to understand the experience of the players, and then finding ways to engage.

Sometimes immersing myself meant talking to those playing, making sure to address them according to the role they were playing, and taking on a role myself. At first I would simply call out, "Help! Somebody save me!" This worked with so many different roles that I didn't have to know much about the specific characters. Spider-Man, Leonardo the Ninja Turtle, guards, rebels, Omega Supreme, and many others have saved me over the years. The more I joined the play in this way, the more I found common themes of saving others, being brave, being strong, and keeping evil at bay. I did not appreciate these elements of gun play when I only watched from the outside.

> I use the term *occupations* for children's everyday activities in the same sense as the field of occupational therapy. The World Federation of Occupational Therapists (2024) defines occupations as "everyday activities people do . . . to occupy time and bring meaning and purpose to life." I use the term to push against the tendency I see in many adults to limit occupational therapy to skills related to academics, such as handwriting and sitting. Children deserve support for all their occupations that bring meaning and purpose to their lives, including play.

Admittedly, I am stepping back to my adult perspective when I talk about the pro-social benefits of gun play. By focusing only on what children might gain from the activity and not the occupation of play itself, we lose sight of the actual children who are engaged in this play. Even talk of the *whole child* often devolves into discussions about addressing children's social-emotional and physical needs while facilitating their cognitive development. It still comes solely from an adult perspective.

Children do learn through play, of course. They gain knowledge, experience, and understanding. From the outside, we as adults assess what aspects of this knowledge and understanding are worthy of being thought of as *learning.* This is what is generally thought of as authentic assessment, which uses children's everyday actions (or occupations, as explained in the sidebar) as evidence for predetermined goals. Typically, many of the indicators in assessment tools use a framework based on academic expectations for older children and then ratchet back those expectations to younger children.

There is nothing inherently wrong with assessing children's play in this way. In fact, in this book I do much the same thing by looking at our understanding of power in society. But it is important to also appreciate children's play for the experience itself, to understand the intrinsic value and not just the outcomes (Vygotsky [1966] 2016). In doing this, we can begin to understand the experience a little bit more. Children don't play to make me feel good about myself as a teacher; they play to feel good about themselves.

To that end, I want to show children's perspective in play. I will use stories from my thirty years in classrooms, as well as several interviews with children and youth reflecting on their pretend play. When I relay stories, I will use the name of the role rather than the child when they are engaged in play and only use their name when they step out of the role. In the introduction, I talked about "the Boss" rather than Maggie when describing the scenario. In each chapter, I also step into my adult perspective with strategies to facilitate children's sense of power.

Othering Gun Play

Many early childhood educators have treated gun play and other imaginary play with violent themes as unconnected to other types of pretend play. I find this thinking problematic. It has resulted in adults worrying about gun play in a way that they don't worry about other types of play. As Michael G. Thompson, one of the authors of *Raising Cain: Protecting the Emotional Life of Boys*, said in a *Huffington Post* article, "Are there correlations between boy [gun] play and adult male violence? I have *never* found a study that connects the two. Likewise, there's no research saying that girls who have their dolls play family and have babies are going to become sexually active at a young age" (Pearson 2019).

Adults' fear of gun play is emotional rather than logical. This is fed by fear of violence from firearms (as opposed to pretend play). The American Medical Association (2024) considers firearm violence to be a public health crisis. It was the leading cause of death for teens as of 2022 (John Hopkins Bloomberg School of Public Health 2024). Although no evidence links this tragic fact to children's pretend play, firearm violence among teens appears to be influenced by real-life experiences, as the Violence Project found that a significant percentage of mass shooters have a history of childhood trauma (The Violence Project 2021).

The othering of gun play creates a sense of fear, which often leads to banning the play and results in power struggles between the children who want to play and the adults who want to ban it. The fact that the vast majority

I use the term *firearm* to refer to real weapons and the term *gun* when referring to play. This is to highlight that children are pretending. When they hold up a finger or a toy and make a shooting sound, they are not, in fact, firing any projectile, and there is no physical harm caused by this play.

of children who engage in gun play are boys and the vast majority of adults who work with young children are women only exacerbates this process of othering. Some children display a strong drive to engage in weapons play and attempts to ban it are fruitless. As Jay Mechling (2008, 202) puts it, "Both scholars and parents noted in frustration that the ban on guns was a hopeless battle, as boys would make guns out of Lego blocks, sticks, plastic '7s' and 'Ls,' and their bare hands."

Banning gun play in group settings is not based on any research in child development or psychology but rather on cultural norms. Yet I do not want to fall into the trap that says gun play equals boy play, or that banning it happens because women don't like it. Some boys don't play this way, but many do. Some girls play this way, but most do not. And some children who do not identify as a boy or a girl play this way while others do not (see chapter three for more on gender identity). Meanwhile, many women do allow children to engage in gun play, both as parents and as care providers in group settings. However, my experience has been that family care providers are more likely to allow gun play than educators who work in child care centers and school-based programs. It seems to me that the more adults there are working together, the more they tend to follow the cultural norm of banning gun play. This is quite similar to how adults in group care often ban roughhousing.

The effect of this is that children who are attracted to gun play can feel that this part of them is not welcome in the group setting. Those with a strong desire to play this way may especially feel unwelcome. This feeling of disconnection can create a feeling of powerlessness within the community. If anything, banning gun play will increase the desire to engage in gun play because it gives children a sense of power, even if only in the realm of their imagination.

Exploring Power

When I began understanding gun play with intention, I would find times to reflect with children soon after play. It struck me that the answers to what princesses do and what superheroes do were almost identical. Princesses and superheroes protect people, save the world, and help sick people. But there are some differences in the way they answer a problem. According to my preschool students, superheroes kill the bad guy and princesses say, "step, kick, spin." But the similarities far outweigh the differences. In each I hear references to protection and nurturance, both roles that adults ideally play in children's lives.

Looking at these roles as taking on adult traits allowed me to connect them to other pretend roles tied more closely to real life, such as Mom, Firefighter, and Doctor. In fact, children often take on roles of power. Children are relatively powerless in their lives, so this makes sense. They are told when to eat, when to clean up, and when to go to bed. They also don't have full context for things beyond their control. Severe weather, fires, illness, and many other situations can be overwhelming, but especially so when children cannot see how some dangers might be mitigated. Adults may know that you cannot shoot a tornado to stop it from destroying your house, but I have seen children play this way after the first tornado drill of the year here in my home state of Minnesota.

My understanding of power in young children has evolved over the years. Early in my career, I focused on fostering independence in children. I helped them learn to put on their shoes and zip their coats. Looking back, I think I was focused on children developing self-care skills because I was focused on what skills or knowledge they lacked, and I saw my role as an educator to impart my knowledge. I didn't truly see children as active participants in their own development. This resulted in me trying to teach children to regulate by telling them what to do or not to do. Essentially, I regulated them hoping they would then learn to regulate themselves.

What I was missing is children's own empowerment. I have since learned to focus on children's autonomy rather than their independence. *Autonomy* focuses on deciding for oneself. *Independence* focuses on doing something on your own regardless of who made the decision. Early in my career, children put on their own boots and jackets because I told them to. This often turned into me badgering some children to stop dawdling and put on their shoes. When I shifted my perspective to autonomy, I focused on our need to wear boots and jackets to stay warm and dry. This slight shift resulted in me asking the children to help each other get ready. Those who could zip gladly went around to those who couldn't. They became more interdependent and consequently more empowered.

Power Play

Gaining a sense of power—of control and agency—is a major part of development for young children. This occurs through their interactions with their imaginations, their growing understanding of themselves, and their experiences with peers and adults. Some of this happens through play, which is my main focus in this book. But children's need to take on roles of power is also influenced by their feeling of agency in the world, so I also explore our roles as adults in group care and how we can foster a child's sense of agency and power.

Each chapter in this book looks at exercising power from a different perspective. Chapter one focuses on what power means to children and how they use it in their play. Chapter two looks at how imagination is central to the empowerment of children. Chapter three explores the way children develop their cultural and gender identity and how this interacts with the power play they engage in. Chapter four looks at the real-life power dynamics between children when they play together. In chapter five, I turn the lens on our actions as adults and how we exercise power with children. And finally, chapter six discusses the need for adults to be empowered so they can nurture children's sense of power in themselves.

We do a disservice to children if we think of them as powerless. Perhaps they are when we view them from our adult world. But if we glimpse inside the world of their imagination, we can see their power is boundless, not in some distant future, but right here, right now, if we only take the time to look.

CHAPTER ONE

Power

"Bam!" I look across the room and Carson is pointing his finger at Jaxson. I approach them to remind them that we don't allow guns at school. I know they know better because I have reminded them several times today, as I have each day. As I repeat the rule, Carson tells me, "It's a candy bammer. Do you want some candy?" Carson bams candy into his own mouth to demonstrate. Unsure of how to react, I politely decline and walk away, wondering how I can get them to stop playing this way.

Reflecting on this incident, I realize Carson and Jaxson were both smiling, although I didn't notice this at the time. My agenda was to enforce the rules, so all I saw was the rule breaking. We see what we look for.

When I started teaching, I bought into the belief that gun play was something to be feared. The center where I worked banned this type of play, and that made sense to me. Our neighborhood was plagued by violence involving firearms. Yet at the same time, I saw children play out things that scared them, such as getting shots at the clinic, so I knew that it also made sense that they might want to play guns. And trying to stop them from playing this way only resulted in them telling me things like "It's a candy bammer." Meanwhile, I was so focused on how I could stop them from engaging in gun play that I was ignoring why they were doing it.

In retrospect, I think banning gun play initially gave me comfort because it gave me some sense of control over the epidemic of firearm violence. I may not be able to end the crisis, but I can do this one small thing. The problem is that I was viewing the play solely from my adult lens, looking at a societal issue. Meanwhile, I was gaining a small sense of control by exerting power over the children. I was trying to protect them rather than empower them. But children have very little power of their own. They rely on adults (and sometimes older siblings) for their basic needs of food and shelter, as well as for their sense of security and emotional well-being. Unfortunately, not every child receives what they need—physically or emotionally—and they cannot provide it for themselves.

Children understand that they have less power than adults when they observe adults in roles of authority. They rely on adults to help them when they can't do something themselves and look to adults when they are hurt or upset. While this can give them a sense of security, children don't always appreciate this adult authority in the moment. A child needs sleep, but that doesn't mean they want to stop playing at bedtime. The same is true for mealtimes or heading to child care. A child may ultimately benefit from or enjoy their next activity, but because they have a rudimentary ability to picture future events, they may not recognize those future benefits. They may struggle to recall an image of playing with a friend at child care once they arrive, especially when the toys they are currently using at home are right in front of them. Therefore, children often battle this authority in the moment. They want to be in charge.

I have engaged in countless hours of pretend play. I am still struck by how many roles children take on that involve some form of power. They can be animals such as lions, bears, sharks, and dinosaurs. They can be people from the community, such as teachers, firefighters, police officers, and, of course, parents. They can also be fictional characters such as superheroes, princesses, magic ponies, and giant robots. Some of these roles are based on experiences and others are based on things from their imagination. Depending on the child, power may be measured in size, strength, speed, beauty, or level of control over others. As children play with others, they may also take on roles where someone else is in charge of them. They may play a cat, a baby, or someone in need of rescue. More likely, they will alternate those roles, taking the lead at times and other times following. Taking on these roles of power allows them to experience power in ways they may not have otherwise.

When I use the term *power* in this book, I am thinking of it in a personal sense rather than in terms of political power. How can a person feel they have some control in their daily life? How can they have agency over the direction their life goes? At the time of the story that opened the chapter, I was an assistant teacher and new in the field. I wanted to be a great teacher, so I was acting the way I thought a teacher should act. I was practicing the adage *fake it 'til you make it*. As I continued to teach, I got to know the children better and I became more attuned to them. I adapted my practice as I learned what resulted in closer connections with the children, as opposed to actions that made the children less engaged and less trusting.

Over time, I went from *pretending* to be a teacher to actually *being* one by gaining agency. Psychologist Albert Bandura's theory of agency identifies three elements of agency: projecting yourself into the future, self-efficacy, and self-regulation (Bandura and Gervais 2017). I projected myself into the future by picturing what I thought a great teacher acted like. Then I gained self-efficacy, my belief that I could become a teacher. I did this by having success engaging with children, watching other teachers be successful and imitating them, and getting encouragement from teachers and families. The more I had success, the easier it was for me to stay regulated in what is a very stressful job.

As I gained confidence as a teacher, I was more able to give up control. As I said, I think I banned gun play to feel a sense of control I didn't necessarily feel otherwise. Gaining confidence meant I didn't have to rely on my idea of a good teacher. Instead, I reflected on what helped me attune to children. I could focus more on understanding how the ways in which I exercised power with children affected their emotions, their engagement, and frankly, their sense of belonging. And this led me to allow gun play in my classroom. When I think of how much control I exerted over children when I was a new teacher, I realize that feeling powerless can make someone more controlling.

Allowing gun play had a noticeable effect on Damian, a four-year-old I worked with. Damian was the child whose name I called out more than the others. I can remember one time seeing the spark in his eyes literally go out as I tried to convince him that the number-recognition card game was going to be fun. My best intentions as a teacher were based on the idea that my job was to impart knowledge to the children. While I had his academic interest in mind, I was failing to respect Damian as a person. I was only seeing part of Damian. I was failing to appreciate his interests. And I think he felt it. He was supposed to join in the card game because I thought he should. When I allowed gun play, my relationship with Damian changed. I noticed that Damian interacted with me more throughout the day. He would poke my arm and hide behind me before smiling up at me. We had conversations about his play and about his family. When I allowed him to express himself in his play, we had a closer connection.

I wanted to see the smiles of children like Damian, as well as Carter and Jaxson from my earlier story. And to do that, I needed to see all aspects of them. I started with simply allowing them to do gun play, but this soon built my appreciation for this play. Once I got over my fear of gun play, I could see it had more in common with children playing lions or princesses than it did with children hurting others. Ultimately, I needed to find ways for them to explore power.

Over my decades of teaching, I have often been struck by how children exert power. Toddlers insist, "I do it," while preschoolers resist cleaning up toys until you jokingly tell them, "Don't clean up the blocks. I want to do it myself," and of course being powerful seems to be the underlying theme in so much of their pretend play. I found Bandura's theory of agency helpful for understanding children's need for power. *Agency* is about an individual's ability to act on their own ideas, while *power* refers to their interactions with others. Children need agency to have power. Similar to the way Bandura's theory of agency includes projecting yourself into the future, I think that imagination is a key component of power. My understanding of power has four elements: agency, self-efficacy, self-regulation, and connection. I will consider each of these elements throughout the book and discuss how they apply to imagination and identity. First, let me illustrate how each of these elements applies to children's power by sharing a story of my own experience as a new parent.

Agency

Two-month-old Remus, who would later identify with they/them pro-nouns, was screaming in my arms. I walked under an apple tree to cool off in the shade on this hot summer day. As soon as we were under the tree, Remus stopped screaming and looked up. Like so many parents, I tried to find ways to calm my baby and noticed patterns in the process. Over the next few weeks, I observed that Remus would cry when they were in bright light and calm down when the light was lower, especially when the colors were also muted. Remus was articulating their needs with the tools they had, in this case screaming.

By six months, Remus would often alert me with vocalizations that were much closer to speech than screams. If they wanted more broccoli, they gestured toward their tray until I scooped out more of the puree for them. Soon, Remus was using words to let me know what they needed. As Remus developed self-care skills as a toddler, they often took matters into their own hands. If the pants I dressed them in were not comfortable, Remus simply changed into their favorite flower-print leggings. Once when I took Remus to a birthday party, they had a melt-down and we had to go home before cake was even served. Once they had had enough of the party, they knew how to use their actions to get me to leave.

By the time Remus was a preschooler, they were usually able to stay calm and tell me what they needed. They would let me know what types of clothes they wanted. They would often ask to go to the lake or the pool and play in the water for hours. As they got older and were diagnosed with autism spectrum disorder, Remus was always part of conversa-tions with teachers about their sensory needs in the classroom. Later, when school staff were creating accommodations plans, Remus always joined their parents at the meetings and spoke up for what they needed for success in the classroom, including wearing a hat and sound-canceling headphones and not sitting directly under the overhead lights.

In the story above, Remus let me know what they needed at every stage of their growth. Agency is "being able to make choices and decisions to influence events and to have impact on one's world" (Australian Children's Education and Care Quality Authority 2018). Even at two months, Remus was deciding they needed to be away from bright lights and communicated this in the only way they could at the time, by screaming. As Remus grew older, they were able to communicate in other ways, through actions, gestures, and speaking, so by the time they were in high school they could self-advocate.

This story is focused on the child exerting control over the environment they are in, in this case the sensory stimuli, but the lessons can be applied to other ways the child has control in their physical and social environment. For example, an infant might crawl to an object they want. A toddler might push a bowl of apple slices away and say, "No!" A preschooler might tell a peer that they want to help build a block tower.

Outside of play, young children don't have agency in many parts of their daily lives. They are told when to eat, when to go to sleep, when to go home, and so on. Of course, there are reasons a child doesn't make these decisions on their own. Many things that children do not want to do in the moment have long-term benefits that might not be obvious at the time. A child does not have all the information or skills needed to decide these things on their own. On the other hand, if a child is not involved at all, the adult may make decisions that are not in the best interest of the child. A child in group care may be hungry before the next meal, for example. The hungry child may then have less ability to regulate their emotions and be more prone to hit or bite.

Over time, most children are able to take a more active role in making decisions that affect their world. This can be facilitated or hindered by the actions of the adults in their life. For a child to gain this sense of agency, they need to believe they can influence their own life. This belief is called self-efficacy.

Self-Efficacy

In the previous story, Remus showed agency by screaming when the sun was too bright. The screaming got me to bring them into the shade. Over time, I learned to adjust the brightness of the room or move Remus whenever they indicated the light was bothering them. Remus let me know, first with screaming, then crying, then whimpering, until they finally used words. At the same time, Remus gained physical agency and could move under a table or find a nook that was dimmer. Remus didn't simply gain agency; they also knew their protestations would result in change.

Self-efficacy and agency tend to work together. As a child gains agency, their belief in their ability to have agency increases. This belief is self-efficacy. Furthermore, high self-efficacy leads to more effort and higher outcomes, and the reverse is true: "Low self-efficacy leads to less effort and lower persistence and therefore lower outcomes, which in turn lead to lower self-efficacy beliefs" (Reyhing and Perren 2021, 2).

Bandura recognizes four ways to increase self-efficacy: finding success in smaller steps of a task; seeing others be successful at something you want to try; getting encouragement from others; and having an awareness of your own emotions and the way those emotions affect your heart rate, breathing, and muscle tension (Bandura and Gervais 2017). As I translate these four ways to increase self-efficacy for early childhood education and care providers, I see strategies that providers can use with the children in their care.

Finding success in smaller steps is akin to scaffolding. We as adults do this all the time for young children. I'm sure I'm not alone in realizing that more children can put their winter gear on if I first ask them to put on their snow pants. Once they have done that, I tell them to put on their boots, then coats, then hats, and then mittens. Eventually they can do all these steps without a reminder at each step, but it happens gradually. I can also provide photos of each step of the process for children to follow along. Other children can also take on this role, scaffolding a variety of tasks for a peer. Children will increasingly break tasks down into steps themselves, but this is a learned skill that adults are integral in fostering.

The next way to increase self-efficacy is to see others being successful at something. Some children spend a lot of time watching others. After watching, they are ready to try themselves. I worked at a small center where crossing the monkey bars was a rite of passage for many. A group of preschoolers would spend hours going back and forth. At first, they would reach one bar and drop down, but gradually they learned to go across all six bars. Then, as they mastered the equipment, they would add challenges like skipping a bar. There was always one child who would stand nearby just watching. They rebuffed any encouragement to try it themselves. After a few weeks, they would finally go up to the monkey bars and go across all six. I was fascinated by these children. They always reminded me that there are many ways to support children in their development. My hunch is that watching allowed them to break down the task into smaller steps. This also required them to imagine (there's that word again) how their own body would need to move, coordinating their upper arms, hands, and feet.

The next method for building self-efficacy is getting encouragement from others. Again, this is another staple in what we do all day with children. This is not simply giving generic praise for a child, like "good job." Nor is it expressing encouragement for everything they do. Alfie Kohn (1993) reminds us that random praise can actually demotivate children. They act for the praise itself rather than feeling intrinsic motivation to master a skill that they have chosen. Encouragement should be specific acknowledgment of what a child did or is about to do. You can acknowledge the actions, the effort, or the emotions the child is experiencing. Again, peers may provide encouragement, and often do so in ways the adult might not.

Finally, children need to be aware of their own emotions and the ways those emotions are experienced in their bodies. This begins at the earliest stages of life. When a very young child feels something unpleasant internally, they cry and, ideally, an adult responds to meet the need. This internal sense is called *interoception* (there is more detail on interoception in chapter four). In their book, *The "Why" Behind Classroom Behaviors*, Jamie Chaves and Ashley Taylor point out that "there is a strong connection between our emotions and physiological responses" (2021, 96). Preschoolers typically master many of the skills necessary for bodily functions or can ask for help (a form of agency). Emotional regulation—especially in terms of understanding one's internal feelings—is usually what children are working on most as preschoolers. A child can learn to recognize that their breathing will get shallower and their heart will race when they are mad, scared, or hurt. There are times when it is a sign of fear of something new, like trying the monkey bars without knowing whether they will be successful. Adults can help them notice these physiological responses and teach them to take deeper breaths to return to stasis. A child can learn that this stress response (increased breathing and heart rate) doesn't automatically mean to stop doing something.

Self-Regulation

Self-regulation allows a child to use power in an intentional way. The term is sometimes used interchangeably with emotional regulation, but self-regulation refers more broadly to the regulation of actions or behaviors that someone might take in reaction to their emotions. For instance, consider what happens when a child asks to use a toy and another child says no. Simply wanting something and taking it by force may seem like power in the short term, but in the long run it can make a person less able to get what they want. In this case, if the child grabbed the toy, they might have the toy in their hands but probably wouldn't be able to play with it because the other child would try to grab the toy back and a conflict would ensue. If the child controls their impulse to grab the toy, they might be able to find a similar toy or another toy that would allow them to play with the other child. If the goal was to play with the toy they wanted to grab, controlling their initial impulse is more likely to result in them playing.

This skill develops gradually in young children (see chapter five for discussion on the adult acting as mediator in conflict resolution). The first step is for a child to express their needs. This expression usually starts with crying. Crying communicates that you need something, but it doesn't allow another to know what is needed. As a child's needs become more complicated, having ways to communicate those needs helps them get those needs met. Thinking back to the story I shared at the beginning of this chapter, Remus was more successful as they gained the ability to stay calm and articulate their needs. They had more power in various situations.

In education fields, the term *self-regulation* sometimes is used to mean merely children's ability to comply. I have seen many individualized education programs (IEPs) that have a self-regulation goal of sitting for circle time for a designated amount of time. This is clearly about compliance rather than the child regulating themselves. In my experience, goals in IEPs are focused on the educators' objectives and not the child's. A goal of true self-regulation would have to consider the child's objective. For example, a child who wants to learn to climb trees needs the self-regulation to not get discouraged with multiple failures before success. It seems reasonable to me that a child's objectives be considered as well as the educators' when developing goals. Rather than simply making a goal for a child to sit at circle time for five minutes, ask the child for an idea of what they think the class should do at circle time and then together make a goal for that child to participate. This meets the educational objective of group participation while motivating the child to participate because they had a voice in the planning.

Another way to look at self-regulation is to think of it as the child's ability to use the right executive function skills at the right time (Center on the Developing Child at Harvard University 2021). The main executive function skills are inhibitory control, mental flexibility, and working memory. These skills are foundational to almost any other social, cognitive, or communication skill, and pretend play fosters the development of these skills. (I will cover strategies to foster executive function skills throughout the book.) These skills are intertwined because each individual skill is reinforced by the development of the other two skills. Here is an overview of these skills and how they relate to children's exploration of power.

Inhibitory control: Impulse control and focus

Inhibitory control includes impulse control and focus. Impulse control is the ability to resist a first impulse and then choose how to react in a situation. If someone bumps me at a grocery store, I may have a knee-jerk reaction to push them back or yell at them. But if I control that impulse, I may consider the broader context and realize that I walked in front of them to reach for the last bottle of my favorite hot sauce. Even this split-second pause allowed me to realize that I may have been paying attention to something else and caused the collision. This is a skill learned over time. Young children are just developing this ability. When I was new in my career, I would admonish a child for pushing back when they were pushed. Early childhood author Dan Hodgins would frequently refer to this as making a moral judgment of a developmental issue. I was reacting to the child pushing as a choice they were making to misbehave rather than understanding that they were still developing the ability to control their impulse to push back.

Impulse control is important for experiencing power because it can lead to delayed gratification. If I want a truck someone is using, I could take it out of their hands, but if I build a road out of blocks, we might play together with the truck and road, making it more fun.

Children playing pretend utilize impulse control when they only use the powers of their character. Elsa can make things freeze but cannot fly. Superman can fly but does not use guns. Children also use impulse control when their pretend play involves roughhousing, something common with certain types of power play such as superhero play. Roughhousing, a type of play that embodies physical power for many children, fosters impulse control by the very nature of the play. Children engaged in roughhousing are motivated to keep the play going. Players use enough force to keep it exciting without actually injuring others. This also requires the players to maintain enough emotional regulation to not react in anger if they do accidentally get injured. Emotional regulation is fostered by allowing this type of play rather than banning it (Huber 2017).

Impulse control develops gradually. I think most children have a sense that delayed gratification is related to power because it often shows up in their play when they take on a parental role with their actual parent (see the power reversal and power amplification section later in this chapter). For example, a three-year-old might take on the role of "Mom" while their real-life mom pretends to be the "Child." For the next ten minutes, "Mom" tells her "Child" to eat all her vegetables before she can have ice cream.

Focus is the ability to filter out most sensory input and only pay attention to needed input. This is how most people are able to hold a conversation in a loud restaurant. Focus is also related to impulse control because it allows children to pay attention to something positive rather than the negative. If a child is building with blocks and gets bumped, they can focus on the building instead of giving into the impulse to push back.

Focus is fostered when children choose their own activities. While children eventually need to learn to focus on nonpreferred activities, they first need to learn to focus on things they enjoy. Power play is highly motivating for most children when they get to embody a character of their own choosing. Giving children time and space to play is an effective way of fostering impulse control and focus. These skills also become easier when a child develops mental flexibility and working memory.

Mental flexibility and working memory

Mental flexibility and working memory typically develop closely together, and I often think of them together. Mental flexibility is thinking through possible ideas or dealing with change. Working memory is the ability to remember necessary information for a task. In a group setting these skills often show up when a child wants to use a material that someone else is using. If Becky sees someone drawing with the only purple crayon she can find, she can be flexible if she can think through her possibilities. The only possibilities she can access are those that she physically sees or what she can picture mentally. Must she use a crayon or can she use paint instead?

Can she picture other parts of her drawing that use other colors and work on those? An adult could ask Becky, "I wonder what else you could use to make your purple dragon?" or even, "Should we look for something else you could use to make your purple dragon?" Compared to adults, children rely more on their physical senses rather than mental imagery. This is easy to forget when working with children. I still catch myself expecting children to remember all the materials in the room. But it is less effective when I only ask what else they could use, without any verbal prompting or moving around looking at what is available. The better I get at walking around with children to look, the less often children simply melt into tears. I remind them, "I think I saw some other things to draw with over here. Let's see if we can find purple."

Because children are just developing these skills, visual supports (often referred to as simply *visuals*) can be helpful. Visuals are photos or drawings that break down the steps of a task or depict materials available for use. A common visual here in Minnesota I have used consistently is a series of photos showing the steps for putting on snow gear. Eventually most children can remember the steps, picturing them in their mind rather than needing an actual picture.

Working memory also affects a child's focus and their ability to stay on task. Sometimes a child has little or no trouble beginning a task such as going to get their boots to go outside, but they get sidetracked along the way. If they stop to talk to a friend, they will have difficulty recalling which step they were on and what to do next. Working memory also helps a person stay on task when there is a setback. A small issue can derail an entire task if the person forgets their original intention. If a child is pretending to make dinner and the toy pizza won't fit in the pan they are using, the child can get so focused on trying to make it fit that they lose sight of the play scenario—making dinner—and just focus on getting the pizza to fit. The child's mental flexibility is diminished if they forget the bigger picture.

Fostering self-regulation and executive function skills

All executive function skills are harder to access when we are upset. All of us have seen a child get so upset that even when a solution seems within reach from our perspective, the child doesn't see it. Becky could have had three purple markers next to her, but she was so completely focused on the specific crayon that she couldn't switch to using the other materials. Teaching children self-regulation skills such as taking deep breaths, hugging, or cuddling with a stuffed animal can help children access these executive function skills. Developing these executive function skills, in turn, can decrease the frequency or intensity of dysregulation.

Pretend play allows children to practice executive function skills at a slightly more mature level than they might otherwise, or as child development theorist Lev Vygotsky ([1966] 2016, 18) put it, when children play, they are "a head taller." When children immerse themselves in a character they tend to stay regulated longer, maybe because they are slightly dissociated from themselves—"I'm not Mike, I'm Omega Supreme." Entering a flow state helps explain this as well (as discussed in chapter two). Children engaged in power play illustrate this beautifully. The children are emotionally regulated even as they embody characters who are in conflict. They are playing out the emotions while not experiencing them. This allows them to use mental flexibility rather than getting stuck in a dysregulated state as they might if it were an actual conflict. Play fighting may worry adults, thinking that children are learning to solve issues by fighting, but it can have the exact opposite result as it improves their executive functioning.

Executive function skills are necessary for critical thinking, problem solving, and executing multistep tasks, so it is important for children to develop these skills and the self-regulation needed to use them. Pretend play helps with this development, but adults can help foster these skills in other ways too. Here is a summary of executive function skills and then a few strategies for fostering them.

EXECUTIVE FUNCTION SKILLS

- **Inhibitory control**
  - **Impulse control** (asking someone to stop instead of hitting them)
  - **Focus** (listening to an adult's voice rather than the ventilation)

- **Mental flexibility**
  - **Thinking through possible ideas** (making choices)
  - **Dealing with change**

- **Working memory** (remembering you are going to put on your boots and coat while you walk over to the coatrack)

STRATEGIES FOR FOSTERING THESE SKILLS

- Impulse control
  - Encourage start-and-stop games like freeze dances and red light/green light.
  - Allow roughhousing that requires using just enough force to keep the game going.

- Focus
  - Provide for long periods of uninterrupted play (both indoors and outdoors) so children focus on something they like doing.
  - Encourage movement to music in such a way that children focus on a single element of the music, like the descending violins in Vivaldi's "Summer."

- Thinking through possible ideas
  - Ask questions such as "What's your plan?" or "What could you do?" to help child engage with materials or peers.
  - Engage in story dictation or storytelling.

- Dealing with change
  - Give verbal reminders before a transition.
  - Display visual messages to alert children to changes in routine or environment and refer back to the messages.

- Working memory
  - Keep a predictable routine so children can internalize what happens next.
  - Organize materials so children can mentally map the environment when looking for an item.

STRATEGIES FOR FOSTERING SELF-REGULATION

- Breathing
  - Introduce strategies for practicing slow, intentional breathing with children during group times such as:
    - Use an expandable breathing ball, opening and closing the ball slowly in time with a slow inhale and exhale.
    - Do yoga regularly so children practice intentional breathing.

- Have children hold up a hand and pretend each finger is a candle and blow out each one, taking a slow breath each time.
- Have children pretend to hold up a flower. Sniff the flower by inhaling through the nose and then blow the petals by slowly exhaling through the mouth.
- Have children blow bubbles, which requires a slow, steady breath.

  ◦ Remind children to breathe using these strategies when they are mildly upset.

- **Take a break**

  ◦ Provide a cozy corner or other space where children can take a break from more sensory-stimulating environments.

  ◦ Keep soft items for cuddling in the area.

  ◦ Provide fidgets in the area.

- **Acknowledge emotions**

  ◦ Say "You seem angry" or "You're ripping up your picture. You seem frustrated."

  ◦ Read books that depict a variety of emotions.

  ◦ Use two puppets to act out stories involving emotions and ask children for ideas for how the puppet could calm down.

  ◦ Over time, add more terms to describe emotions more specifically (start with *mad* and later use *frustrated*, *irritated*, and *furious*).

- **Touch or proximity**

  ◦ Give hugs and let children sit on your lap.

  ◦ Sit nearby children who don't want direct touch.

  ◦ Regularly read to children one-on-one with them on your lap or next to you.

Connection

Power is social, something exchanged between people (Kok, Loeber, and Grin 2021). Children often play out power roles in the company of others and seem to look for acknowledgment of the power they are inhabiting. The toddler roars like a lion and then smiles when an adult responds, "Wow, what a loud roar!" A preschooler tells a peer, "I'm the mom," and they smile at each other when the peer says they are the baby.

The power dynamics in social interactions can be broken down into three basic types. Educator Eve Trook referred to these dynamics as power exercised *on*, *for*, or *with* a child.

> Power exercised ON a child means the child has no choice. . . . Power exercised FOR a child means that the child is provided experiences that contribute to the development of self-esteem and confidence that lead to power for the child. . . . Power exercised WITH a child means that the teacher and the child are equals learning together, and the child acquires new power. (Trook 1983, 2)

I find the term *power over* is more descriptive than *power on*, but otherwise I find Trook's framework helpful in looking at group dynamics in early childhood. Trook was referring specifically to the ways adults interact with children in a group setting, but children also exercise these same dynamics in their interactions with peers. This happens in both the realm of imagined play and the real world interactions of the children playing. In this chapter (and chapter two), I am focused on how children exercise power within the world of play. I will explore the ways in which children exercise power with one another in real life in chapters four and five.

Power over

The roles in power play often exert power *over* others. This can be a simple game such as bear chase or more complex such as Elsa and Olaf rescuing Anna from Prince Hans, reenacting part of the movie *Frozen*. Sometimes this play can include killing an enemy. This can get uncomfortable for adults who have a different understanding of death than young children. Yet this has long been part of folklore and stories for children: the billy goats kill the troll, Dame Gothel turns to dust when Rapunzel is freed, countless dragons are slain.

Keep in mind that much of this play is exaggerated and that death is not a permanent condition in the minds of most young children. Aretha may pretend to be a lion eating up her dad, but she is not imagining her father actually being consumed, nor is she imagining his demise. This type of play is usually accompanied by smiles and laughter from both parties precisely because it is so removed from reality. Play that reverses the power dynamic can foster bonding. The dad has more power than his daughter, but in the game, the "Lion" has all the power over the victim. The dad, in this case, is relinquishing power and the child is wielding it. There needs to be a level of trust for this play. The dad needs to have enough self-efficacy of his own to relinquish power even if it is in a playful way. Aretha needs to trust that if a real crisis happens, such as a scraped knee, her dad will reassert his power to tend to the injury. When this trust exists, power reversal play can be enjoyable for both players.

Power reversal play differs from play with peers. It's been my experience that when a person of authority is involved, whether it is a parent/family member, care provider, or babysitter, the power element is at its most exaggerated. As a preschool teacher, I am frequently locked up in jail, poisoned, and inoculated. There is no end to the amusement of playing these simple scenarios over and over. Sometimes this power reversal play can be a little subtler, such as when I take on the role of power but they subvert it. Children will ask me to be the dad, but then my kids run away instead of going to bed and I have to chase them. They also ask me to "be the teacher" and then run away or put me in jail. The fact that they ask me to be the teacher when I am their teacher in real life tells me they are trying to be clear that this is play. The exaggeration in play is significant in making this distinction. In real life, they might get annoyed when I tell them to clean up for rest time. But when they are pretending, they poison me and run away. The children are "ensuring that they . . . win" (Jones and Cooper 2006, 64). They trust me to know that my role is letting them win.

Play with peers often involves having power over others, but because the real-life power differential is missing, it looks different. There is still difference in the real-life power and the imaginary power. In group play, often there is one role of power and several others that are subjected to this power. When playing family, there is usually one mom (I rarely see two-parent families in preschoolers' pretend) and then any number of babies, big brothers, big sisters, and cousins. The same is true for roles such as doctor, queen, king, bear, and so on. There is an established hierarchy with one person in charge.

Superhero, princess, and gun play is less hierarchical when considered through this lens of power differentials. These scenarios often only have roles of power with no one taking on a less powerful role. Sometimes players take on roles that vie for the same power: in other words, they battle in some way. This may involve play fighting, shooting, sword fighting, or rough-housing. This gets uncomfortable for some adults, but again, the players trust one another enough to exchange power in the imaginary realm. This play is exaggerated, removing it from real-life situations. Two children may happily agree to play Ninja Turtles, but the play itself is Leonardo battling Shredder as sworn enemies. The two dynamics are completely separate, and children do not confuse the two even if adults sometimes do.

Make-believe also explores finding power over fear. In this case the players might all work on the same side, such as in princess or superhero play. Sometimes one player takes on the role that induces fear. Unlike family play that often involves one person remaining in the powerful role through-out, fear play often involves a transition of power. Predator/prey games are an example of this. Sometimes these fears come from lived experience. I will explore this further in chapter two.

Kylie Cooper, an educator who has studied fear play, told me, "It's important for children to know how to get in and out of fear play" (pers. comm., February 7, 2024). Children gravitate to this play because fear can be overwhelming in real life. "During play, a child can reclaim power over fear. In a sense, it is a way to say, 'I know this feeling. I know how to navigate it,'" Cooper noted. She has watched her two-and-a-half-year-old daughter explore fear by playing bears. Here is how Cooper described it:

She held up her hands like claws and told me she is a bear. I show my scared face and say, "Oh no, a bear!" I ran away just fast enough to stay ahead for a few steps. She growled and chased after me. After a min-ute or so, she said, "I'm a friendly bear." I gave her a hug and told her I love her bear hugs. But soon she announced, "Now I'm a scary bear. You have to run!" So, I screamed and ran away. Before I knew it, she told me that I'm a scary bear, so I growled and chased her. Of course, I didn't catch her unless she slowed down, which told me she wanted me to catch her.

At first glance, the game seems repetitive, but each time is a little different. She tries on different roles. She sometimes growls louder or stomps but then she quickly switches to being a friendly bear.

Or sometimes she will say that a bear is chasing both of us, so we run together and then cuddle up somewhere. I get to watch her going in and out of the scary role just like I wrote in my capstone [thesis] a decade ago. She always maintains a play face, so I know she's not actually overwhelmed. Even if she is pretending to be angry, you can see her face is relaxed. Because she's a toddler, she only stays in the scary role for a little bit each time, but I can see her push it a little bit each time.

In this play, Cooper's daughter is in control of the play itself. She has power over the play. But in her imagination, she is sometimes the bear exerting power over her mom and other times the bear is after her, and there are times when she shares power with her mom. Fear is an abstract concept, but pretending allows her to embody the emotion and experience it in scaled-down bits. She experiences manageable amounts of stress in this play, which makes her more resilient when she experiences fear in real life.

Children still engage in play that involves fear, but as they get older, the play becomes more complex, involving multiple players and details. Some scenarios will still be in the realm of fantasy, such as superhero or princess play. Other scenarios will be based on lived experiences that cause fear. A young child playing doctor will focus on the details of a checkup that were scariest, often getting (or giving) shots. A child who has other scary experiences, such as an MRI, may also include that in their play.

Fear play can also be unique to a particular child. I once worked with a child, Oakley, who had strong emotions around food. He did not like to try new food and would get quite upset when he couldn't have his favorites. I was pretending with a few other children. They were making dinner. One child crawled over and meowed, so I asked the cooks for some cat food. Oakley crawled over as well. I asked, "Did you want some food, kitty?" He nodded and I put a block in a bowl and gave it to him. For the next twenty minutes, Oakley repeatedly brought over the bowl and then crawled a few feet away. Each time, I put the bowl next to him and said, "Here you go, kitty." The next day, Oakley joined us again. This time he used the food cartons and pretended to cook food that I would eat. Again, this play lasted for at least twenty minutes. As Elizabeth Jones and Renatta M. Cooper (2006, 65) put it, "Make-believe play is their weapon against their real fear of dangers known and unknown."

Power for

Children also exercise power *for* others in their pretend play when they take on a powerful role to benefit someone else. This can also involve power reversal, such as a child who pretends to be a doctor with an adult as the patient. Returning back to Aretha playing with her dad, Aretha can wrap a bandage on his arm instead of being a lion eating him up. This type of power reversal requires trust in much the same way it does when a child exerts power over the adult. It may be easier for the adult to take on this type of role because it doesn't leave them as vulnerable: there are times in real life when adults rely on medical staff or other experts for assistance. Pretending to be helped is easier than pretending to be harmed.

Exploring this type of power contributes to healthy social development. Taking care of others often involves helping someone when they can't help themselves. In real life, children are often the recipients of this care. Taking on this role in play gives them experience in being the grown-up. They also enjoy taking on this role in real life, and with adult help they can find many opportunities to do so, as discussed in chapter five.

As children play more socially, they may simultaneously exercise power *over* one character and power *for* another. They might be a fairy using magic to make a monster disappear to save another fairy. The type of power dynamic may even shift during a scenario. A mom may be ordering her children around as if they were Cinderella one minute and then read them a bedtime story the next. There are no distinct lines between these dynamics, and children easily slide from one to another in the same way they can slide between pretending and the real world.

Shifting our focus away from the play, we can see that children often exercise power for peers by helping less experienced players. Aretha might take on the role of Mom to direct most of the play, which requires multiple skills. While they are playing Baby and Kitty, Dallas and Finn just need to follow Aretha's lead. Mom may exert power *over* Baby and Kitty, but Aretha exerts power *for* Dallas and Finn.

Power with

Finally, children often exercise power *with* others in their pretend play. Cooper and her daughter shared power with each other when they fled the pretend bear. A few children may act as firefighters putting out fires throughout the room. Some children may even form teams where a child works with a few others to try to overpower another group. Han Solo, Princess Leia, and Chewie might take on a group of Stormtroopers. This type of play can easily be mistaken for children actually fighting, but it requires quite a bit of negotiation and collaboration. Chapter four offers a more nuanced discussion of the ways peers share power with one another in power play.

Breaking down power into the four elements of agency, self-efficacy, self-regulation, and connection allows us to understand and appreciate children's pretend play with power in the context of their growth and development. Children need ways to experience agency in which they make decisions that affect their world, even if it is imaginary. They build their self-efficacy when their choices in what to play are validated. Pretend play is uniquely suited to developing self-regulation because children act out emotions while staying in the confines of the play scenario. This sustained play offers opportunities for them to develop their executive function skills of inhibitory control, mental flexibility, and working memory.

Pretend play also brings preschoolers together. When one or two start playing family or superheroes, others are drawn to the play. These connections offer children opportunities to explore all three types of power dynamics: power *over*, power *for*, and power *with* others. Young children learn about power dynamics in the world but also develop their own sense of power. Children need to be active participants in our group care settings to become empowered.

Nowhere does this show up more than in imaginary play. Truly, there is power in pretend. In some ways, I think imagination is the root of power for all of us. Imagination is often thought of as divorced from the real world, but every scientific innovation, every piece of artwork, and every element of society began in someone's imagination. This is just as true in early childhood development. Imagination is how children create their identity, their sense of who they are.

CHAPTER TWO

Imagination

"Princess, come sit on your throne." The princess (Sarah) comes over and sits next to the other princess (Q) on the child-sized couch, both children regally holding their heads high. Suddenly, Han Solo (Josh) and Chewbacca (Patrick) run over and yell, "Get out! This is our Millennium Falcon!" Soon the four are arguing. I come over to help them calm down enough to talk through their conflict. Josh tells Sarah to go play somewhere else. Sarah tells Josh the same thing. Then Q chimes in, "Well, I'm Princess Leia, and this is Queen Amidala and—" Before Princess Leia can finish, Han Solo and Chewbacca (Josh and Patrick) swing into action. Han Solo (Josh) tells the others, "Let's get away from the Stormtroopers!" Princess Leia and Queen Amidala (Sarah and Q) stay on the couch while Han Solo and Chewbacca (Josh and Patrick) sit on the floor in front of them, steering their spacecraft.

Pretending involves mental imagery, the act of perceiving something internally. In the story above, I imagine Sarah looks around and sees a gilded palace where she is sitting on a luxurious throne. Meanwhile Josh and Patrick see the Lego Millenium Falcon from Patrick's house. What I find most intriguing is what Q (who uses they/them pronouns) might be perceiving, given that they are straddling two different play schemes, which must be some kind of an amalgamation of princess play and Star Wars. Q is taking on two perspectives simultaneously. Perspective taking allows children to share common mental imagery, fostering connection during the play. Josh and Patrick did not play with Sarah or Q often, but in the above scenario, they played for over an hour. In play, children often enter a flow state that involves their whole body. This embodied nature of pretend play allows them to sink deeply into their imagined worlds.

Pretending is imagining shared with friends, and it fosters all four elements of power. Children foster their agency and consequently their self-efficacy because each child has the ability to change the imagined world. Sharing the time and space of this make-believe world connects the players in a way that other play does not. Meanwhile, children develop their self-regulation skills due to the immersive nature of the play. Young children's experience of power is intertwined with their imagination.

Mental Imagery

Mental imagery can use any of the senses. The term *visual imagery* is often used interchangeably with mental imagery, but not all people's imagery is visual. In addition, our mental imagery can involve a variety of senses. In my observations, it seems like children often use multiple senses when imagining. But people of all ages use mental imagery. Bandura's theory of agency notes that a person imagining themselves in the future is the first step in achieving their goal. I think this works differently for young children. Their imagery is less bound by time, and their understanding of time is very different from an adult's. The term *yesterday* can mean any moment before now and *tomorrow* can mean a few minutes into the future or it can mean months from now. They might project themselves a few minutes into the future when they create something, seeing the finished tower as they build. But they aren't generally able to imagine themselves a few days or weeks into the future. Instead, they project themselves as something other than themselves with little regard to time.

Unlike adults, young children don't just picture an imagined world—they embody it, live it. Their movements, costumes, tone of voice, and word choice are all affected by this mental imagery. We can only observe these outward expressions of what is mostly internal. This is one reason banning gun play or any other play theme is counterproductive. Adults can only stop the outward expression of something a child is exploring internally. It leaves the child grappling with the ideas without others' involvement. Adults are simply taking themselves out of the conversation. Allowing this play gives us a window into the child's imagination.

Of course, we can't fully know what a child is imagining. We have no way of knowing what a child is visualizing when they pretend. Monsters could look like anything. Children playing together each visualize the monster differently. Even when children are pretending to be characters from a visual medium like movies or picture books, it does not guarantee that the child is visualizing the character in the same way. I had a child who played Toy Story with other children. He would take on the role of Woody, Buzz, or Rex. He knew how to act and what to say in the various roles. It was only after talking to his parents that I found out that he had never watched TV or movies or used a computer, so his only exposure to Toy Story was playing with other children. He may have known what some of the characters looked like, but the way he immersed himself into the world of the movie still makes me wonder what he was picturing when he played.

This points to a larger phenomenon that I have noticed over the years, that each group of children creates their own shared world of pretend play scenarios. One year it was kitty families, dragons, Frozen, and bakery. Another year it was Grandma, kitty orphans, Transformers, and Tinker Bell. Over the months, children might dive into other worlds, but there were typically a few that they would fall back on repeatedly. Most children would have their favorite scenario but also would join the other worlds at times. Almost all children would seamlessly join a play scenario knowing how to act and what to say. I am sure that if we were able to project each child's mental imagery, the characters and settings would not actually match. There is a shared manifestation of a narrative even if the imagery is not shared. In other words, each child knows how to act, speak, or dress for the role, but the way they picture the scene varies.

Getting to these shared narratives requires negotiation. There may be one or two children who have the strongest voices in choosing play, but even those children have to choose scenarios in which others can find roles. There have to be multiple entry points for children to join, whether it is based on individual interests, how physically active the child is, or the prior knowledge needed. There may need to be more entry points if children come from a variety of cultures than if they are from the same culture. You as the adult may need to help outliers find entry points. You may need to tell stories or read books that could fuel collaborative pretend play. What you are doing is giving children scripts to follow if they want to join. These scripts differ from the script from a play or movie. They don't tell a child what to say word for word. Rather, they have some basic guidelines. Darth Vader is evil and talks in a scary voice. Ariel lives in the sea but wants to live on land.

Over the years, the shared narratives in my classroom have varied in name but the underlying themes have been relatively consistent. There are always roles of power and roles of comfort. These roles sometimes mirror the children's experiences and other times offer windows into magical worlds of their minds. All of these themes overlap and intertwine without distinct categories. They are more of a spectrum than a binary, with lived experience at one end and fantasy at the other end.

Lived experience refers to situations the child has experienced directly or witnessed. It can be day-to-day experiences such as doing laundry or making dinner. It can be an event that happens periodically, like a birthday or visit to the clinic. Some of the play will be reliving moments that are comforting for a child. Other times may be moments that caused heightened emotions. It could be something happy like Grandma visiting, or it could be sad or scary like the death of a family pet. Traumatic events, either experienced directly or witnessed by a child, may show up in pretend play. A child may repeat this play as they try to assert control over the situation, similar to the fear play discussed in chapter 1.

Fantasy refers to impossible experiences that can only exist in the imagination (or movies), such as playing superheroes or unicorns. Fantasy play allows children to create as many or as few rules as they want for their play, not bound by reality. This type of play can also involve comfort or strong emotions. The fantasy aspect allows children to explore generalized or even specific fears in an indirect way. If a child is scared of going to the dentist, facing a monster in their play may give them a chance to explore their own bravery. If you can face a monster, maybe you can face the dentist. This removal from a specific situation may make it easier to face some emotions tied to trauma. It's impossible to know why a child may seem obsessed with a particular scenario, but it may be giving them some comfort or healing for something hidden to all but the child.

Most pretend play tends to be somewhere in the middle of lived experience and fantasy. For example, the floor is lava is a game that shows up every few years. Lava does exist, but I'm not sure I have ever worked with a child who has seen it in real life, and I even know very few who have seen video of it. And working with young children, I have seen a wide variety of things end up on the floor but never lava. Movies typically fit somewhere in the middle of this spectrum too. Children experience a movie, but they also might know the situations or characters depicted don't exist in the real world. But of course that doesn't stop them from talking about the characters as if they are real. It's not exactly that children don't know the difference between pretend and reality, but that they can emotionally react to both.

Pretend play also allows some children to rely on their visual imagery to *see* objects in the real world differently. Vygotsky described this as the ability to separate the "visual and meaning fields" ([1966] 2016, 8). As a child, when I would play doctor, I would pick up a peg to give my sister, Suzanne, a shot. My younger sister Jeanine would pick up the same peg to feed her baby a bottle. In this case the baby was actually a feather pillow she named Georgia. Pretending allows children to see the world in a way that matches what they are imagining. The actual prop, the peg in this case, only needs one attribute to match their imagination. Jeanine and I both needed something small and cylindrical. Jeanine's pillow became her baby because it was soft and huggable. Reflecting back, I think we saw the elements we needed and ignored the elements we didn't. Using props is based on children's lived experience but it is not tethered to it.

In addition, this spectrum of lived experience and fantasy applies to both the characters and the setting. I look at these as two different axes with *setting* as the *x*-axis and *characters* as the *y*-axis. A dragon family eats breakfast. Dragons are fantasy but eating breakfast is an experience children have. The reverse could be true, such as playing family on the moon. Of course, children often move between these, so children might be playing family when one of them decides to be Rainbow Dash. The group may shift into My Little Pony or the others may not agree and the child can decide to play elsewhere or go back to family play.

Of course, the lived experiences of some children may seem to be fantasy to others. One child may think of gun play as something that only exists in a world far away. Another child may have a parent in the military who uses firearms for their job. Another child may have a family member who has been injured by a firearm. A tornado may seem like a supernatural power to some, while others have experienced seeking shelter or seen the aftermath of one.

In other words, a pretend play scenario may be a mirror for one child and a window for another. Rudine Sims Bishop (1990) introduced the terms *mirrors*, *windows*, and *sliding glass doors* to discuss how children see their lives represented in various settings. A *mirror* is something that reflects an aspect of who the child is. A *window* depicts a cultural experience that is new to the child. *Sliding glass doors* are ways that children can immerse themselves in cultures other than their own, books that have children emotionally connecting with a character from a different culture. The child immerses themselves in the world of the character as they listen to the book. A picture book about Lunar New Year that shows pictures of how it is celebrated might offer a window into another culture for a child who does not celebrate the holiday. For example, the book *Sam and the Lucky Money* (Chinn 1995) depicts a child trying to decide how to spend the money he got for the New Year. The reader joins the world with the smell of firecrackers, the sound of the gongs, and the feel of the cold winter air.

Pretend play is immersive, but it differs from a picture book. The author of a picture book can provide multiple elements to bring children into the world of the story that the child would have no way of knowing before reading the book. Pretend play originates in the creative imagination of a child, so a child playing alone would not have a realistic understanding of a culture outside their own. However, when children from two different cultural perspectives play together, there are opportunities for each child to act out scenarios that go beyond their lived experience. The difference could just be a detail or two. A child playing from a single-parent family might play with a child from a two-parent family, for example. I give an example of a more immersive experience when I discuss cultural identity development in chapter three.

Perspective Taking

Whether a child is acting out a real-life scenario or something completely fantasy, they are imagining a different world from the here and now. They also are taking on a role other than the person they are in the here and now, meaning they are taking on a perspective other than their own. Perspective taking in pretend play does not just involve a child imagining experiences different from their own. The embodied nature of the play means the child takes into account how to move, which words to use, what tone of voice to speak with, and so on. They have to fully understand the perspective of the character of their role to do this.

This ability to take the perspective of others is primarily a cognitive process that shares some of the same qualities as empathy (Stietz et al. 2019). *Empathy* refers to understanding another person's feelings. At a work meeting about a new project, you might detect a person is nervous or overwhelmed when they address the group. Perspective taking is imagining another person's experience that is different from your own to better understand them. You might remember the person speaking is a single mother and might be worried about arranging child care if the new project involves working overtime. When perspective taking and empathy coordinate, it can allow a person to be prosocial. Feeling the emotions of someone else and then being able to take their perspective allows a person to respond in a way that is helpful to that person. When feeling someone's emotions and perspective taking don't happen in tandem, however, the result may be unhelpful. For example, someone could understand the perspective of another but not consider their emotions and then take advantage of that person. Or someone could rush to try to fix someone's problem because they seem sad, but make the problem worse if they don't understand the other's perspective—such as the well-meaning parent who rebuilds the block castle hoping to stop their child from crying, only to bring the child back to tears because they didn't get to build it.

I bring up this difference because I know that one of the reasons I didn't allow gun play when I first started teaching was that I worried about children learning that they could solve problems with firearms in real life. To put it another way, I worried that they would grow up to be prone to violence and lack empathy for others. I thought they would disregard the feelings of others and see violence as the only way out of conflict. I didn't consider that I also engaged in gun play frequently in my own childhood and grew up resolving conflicts peacefully. I somehow saw my middle-class suburban childhood as unrelated to the lower-income urban neighborhood these children were living in. I failed to see that they might have the same needs for exploring power that I did at their age. Ironically, by disregarding their perspective, I was missing how they were learning the skill of perspective taking in this type of play.

When I first started allowing gun play, I would explain to families that I wanted children to learn empathy by taking on other roles. If they could pretend to be a bad guy, someone antithetical to the way most children view themselves, then they would learn to consider the feelings of people different from themselves. Upon reflection, I am not convinced that empathy is learned from pretend—but perspective taking is. Children embody the role they take on, adapting their movements, actions, and interactions with peers taking on other roles. Meanwhile, children practice empathy in real-life situations, as when an infant cries when another infant cries. The difference may seem insignificant, but I think it deepened my appreciation for the prosocial lessons children take from pretend play, even when it has violent themes.

Letting go of the idea that children learn empathy from pretending makes it easier for me to witness seemingly violent imaginary situations without imposing a real-world lens: Moms putting babies in the oven, fairies casting a spell to make the bad guys disappear, or the superhero blasting a villain. When I instead view these types of pretend play as perspective taking, I worry less about the surface lesson or appearances of what the children were pretending. I am not worried about a child growing up and putting their actual baby in an oven. Instead, I can appreciate that the child is exploring the power a parent has over their child in a very exaggerated way. The child is emotionally regulated in real life when they play this way, even if the character is not.

As these examples of exaggerated power demonstrate, perspective taking starts with very broad strokes, often good guys and bad guys. There is little nuance necessary. In my experience, children view characters as archetypes that do not change. Even when a movie portrays a character with some nuance, such as Elsa from *Frozen* who causes harm when she tries to grapple with her powers, children's play glosses over those nuances. I have only seen young children enact Elsa as powerful and good. This pattern holds true for other characters as well, as they are typically perceived as either good or bad. There is no room for nuance or growth for an individual character. Children simply switch the role they are playing if they want to switch from "good" to "bad."

Flow State

This ability to switch in and out of roles is facilitated by the state of mind children enter when immersed in pretend play, "an alert, active but relatively nonstressed frame of mind," or what has been described as a flow state (Gray 2015, 125). This flow state describes the way children's "perception of 'self' merges with their execution of actions, and their understanding of the passage of time is distorted" (Pavlas 2010, 21). Children imagining themselves in roles of power can shift perspectives fluidly without disrupting the play. In the following vignette, Jamie, Fernando, and Amir play Transformers. Early in the day, the children had their first tornado drill of the year, and it factors in their play. Over the duration of the play, the children play with all three types of power dynamics from chapter one: *over*, *for*, and *with* others. On the surface the scenario is about a superhero and bad guy trying to exert power *over* the other. But in real life the children are exerting power *with* each other, negotiating the play and consenting to the way it goes. Playing in the flow state, the children easily trade off in their power dynamics.

Jamie tells Fernando that she is Bumblebee and Fernando is Megatron, Bumblebee's nemesis. Fernando agrees and the two jump around, moving their arms and legs and making sounds imitating machines, cars, and guns. Bumblebee (Jamie) chases Megatron (Fernando) in the classroom. They match each other's speed, staying about three feet away from each other. After looping around the room once, Megatron (Fernando) turns around and holds out his arm, blasting Bumblebee (Jamie). Bumblebee falls over. "You got me. But I still have power!" Bumblebee holds up her arm and blasts Megatron, who falls down.

Bumblebee calls out "Transform," and crawls away making a car sound. Megatron repeats, "Transform," and crawls after. He blasts Bumblebee again. Amir rushes over, "I'll save you Bumblebee! I'm Cliffjumper!" He blasts Megatron. All three are laughing as all three are making blasting noises and jumping around.

Then Bumblebee (Jamie) crawls under a table. "Oh no, I'm trapped!" Jamie steps out of her Bumblebee role and tells Fernando, "You be Optimus Prime." Fernando nods and in his Optimus Prime voice, turns to Cliffjumper (Amir) saying, "We have to save Bumblebee!"

Optimus Prime (Fernando) and Cliffjumper (Amir) pull at the chairs pretending they are difficult to move. Optimus Prime shouts, "Cliffjumper, use your cannon!" Cliffjumper holds out his arm, "Boom!" Bumblebee pushes the chairs out of the way and scrambles.

Then Bumblebee says, "Oh no, a tornado!" Optimus Prime commands, "Everyone, blasters on!" Jamie steps out of her role and addresses the other children and adults in the room. "Don't worry, we'll kill the tornado!" They continue playing.

In the previous scenario, Jamie is exercising power *for* Fernando, assigning a role for him. This does not mean that Fernando has no agency. He can disagree with Jamie's idea. In this case, Jamie assigned a role that she knew Fernando had done before and seemed to enjoy. Sometimes, a child will take on the role suggested with full agreement. Other times, they may accept a role simply to keep the play going.

Most of the play in this scenario showed the three children exercising power *with* one another. They were all consenting to the way the play is proceeding. Even when they were chasing, they matched one another's pace, indicating they are playing with each other. If one child were trying to get away from the other, they would show signs of distress and run faster. Chapter four discusses these interpersonal dynamics in more detail.

Meanwhile, the power dynamics exercised by the roles of Bumblebee, Megatron, Cliffjumper, and Optimus Prime change throughout the play. At the beginning, Bumblebee and Megatron are each trying to exert power *over* the other by chasing and shooting each other. They each pretend to be shot, allowing the other character to exert power *over* them.

The power dynamics switched when Cliffjumper joins to rescue Bumblebee, exerting their power *for* Bumblebee while also exerting power *over* Megatron. When Optimus Prime joins the rescue, they exercise power *with* Cliffjumper and power *for* Bumblebee. Finally, all three exhibit power *with* one another to have power *over* the tornado. When Jamie announces that they are "killing the tornado," she is demonstrating power for the entire group even though the others are not necessarily part of the game.

Jamie, Fernando, and Amir were immersed in their play. They all seemed to be in a flow state that not only allowed them to each switch their own role but also saw them adapting their understanding of the shifting roles of their playmates. This happens so naturally that I didn't always appreciate the sophistication of children engaging in superhero or gun play. I can think of dozens of children in my career who struggled to stay on task when cleaning up from lunch but could play Spider-Man for over an hour. Earlier in my career, I would have said those children had short attention spans. Now I can see that their attention is dependent on whether they are in a flow state. If my goal is to increase their attention span, I need to give them longer periods of time to engage in pretend play and feel that flow. This flow state allows children to practice executive function skills for a sustained period, including perspective taking, mental flexibility, inhibitory control, working memory, and self-regulation.

The perspective taking used in pretending requires a child to focus on the actions their character would do and filter out other actions. If you are a cat, you crawl around and meow. You don't walk on two feet or speak. If you are a bad guy, you don't do good things. Children set boundaries rather than rules in this play to control certain behaviors. Being in the flow state encourages children to practice staying within these boundaries for an extended period of time—an exercise in impulse control as well as perspective taking.

Being in the flow state during pretend play supports the self-regulation needed for children to practice mental flexibility. Even when the situation is imaginary, children seem to experience some of the same somatic reactions (increased heart rate, shallow breathing) as a real-life situation. At the same time, they can step out of the role if it gets overwhelming (Kylie Cooper, pers. comm.).

Mental flexibility is demonstrated in several ways during pretend play. At any time, a group of children may change the boundaries and expectations of play to include other children or new ideas, using mental flexibility. Interacting with children of different abilities fosters a child's mental flexibility and social skills. A group of children playing aliens might all be speaking in robotic voices, but they may allow a child playing cat nearby to join and meow. Children will also give instructions for minor mistakes in following the expectations of the role, for example, "You have to crawl if you're a cat."

Because pretend play is embodied mental imagery, a child may imagine actions that they cannot actually do in real life. A child cannot fly, but when they pretend to be a Pegasus, they need to think of ways to mimic flying, exercising mental flexibility. It might be flapping their arms like wings or making a whooshing noise to indicate speed. The collaborative nature of most pretend play also means that multiple ideas will be involved. Even if one Pegasus wants to fly to the top of a volcano, another Pegasus may want to go to Pegasus school. The two will now have to change what they were picturing. A simple prompt from the educator may be enough to support their problem solving. "You want to fly to a volcano, and they want to go to school. I wonder what you could do?" Of course, these disagreements can lead to a heated conflict, in which case you may need to help them co-regulate before problem solving.

In my experience, I have observed that children exercise more mental flexibility when conflict arises. I think it's for two reasons. The first is that the imaginary nature of the play allows for more possibilities since solutions don't have to be grounded in the real world. The second is that children are motivated to stay in the flow state so they may accept a solution even if it's not exactly what they wanted. During these conflicts, children have to remember what other possibilities there are, whether that means physical props in the room they might use or scenarios they might follow. As mentioned in the previous chapter, the process of keeping in mind other information while engaged in a task is referred to as working memory. Working memory can help a child stay in a flow state because it allows them to adjust their ideas to keep the play going. The adult can support children in this by asking what other scenarios they could play or by reminding them of what they have played in the past.

A child who struggles to stay in character or seems limited in the scenarios they can play may find themselves excluded. An adult can help this child in gaining this skill. You may be able to simply be nearby and remind them of what the role is. "Do you remember what a kitty does?" It might be helpful to take on the same role so you can model the actions. "Meow. Remember, we are cats, so we meow. What else do cats do?" It may also help if you play one-on-one with the child so they can develop the skills. You can follow their ideas and occasionally stretch their thinking with phrases such as, "I wonder what would happen if . . ." If you see a child watching play who seems to be at a loss for how to join, you can narrate with them. What are the roles the players are enacting? What other roles would make sense?

This modeling can go two ways. If a child is limited in their impulse control, you may also need to remind the other children: "He doesn't always remember to meow like a cat. But he is still following you, so I think he still wants to play. (Turning to child) Do you still want to be the cat? Do you want to be something else in the game?" I do want to stress that we must attune to the child when helping children join pretend play. Just because most preschoolers like to participate in group pretend play does not mean a specific child does. Not all children engage in pretend play, and it is only a deficit if they want to but don't have all the skills needed to join. On the other hand, if the same child has made a few failed attempts or it seems like they want to join but don't know how, you can offer to pretend with them.

Imagination and Power

Imagination allows children to explore power they may or may not have in real life. Young children project themselves into a world where they can have an impact, indeed a world that only exists because they have dreamt it up. This world can change simply because they want it to change. Young children's projections are not bound by time or the limits of the physical world. Breaking down power into the elements of agency, self-efficacy, self-regulation, and connection, we can see how exercising imagination through pretend play is uniquely suited to children's exploration of their own power.

Agency

Adults can increase their sense of agency by projecting themselves into a future state, according to Bandura's model of agency. These projections are imaginary but grounded in reality. I imagined myself to be a published author long before I became one. This allowed me to identify what steps I could take to do this, first writing for the parent newsletter and later for magazines until I started writing book proposals. Young children, on the other hand, project themselves into a future state that is less grounded in real-world details. A young child might take on a caring role such as a dragon curling up to their baby dragon to sleep. They might take on a role of protection like a superhero catching a bad guy. The role might be wholly fantasy, but taking on real-life roles of caring and protection is realistic. Children are projecting roles where their actions affect others, the very definition of agency.

As the adult, you can foster this exploration by giving children plenty of time, space, and materials to explore agency. If a child is struggling to join pretend play, play with them so they can practice the skills. As the child gets more comfortable with pretending, include other children. If there is a difference in culture, ability, or experience between children that is acting as

Many adults show a preference for spoken language. This preference colors the way many view gun play and superhero play, which often relies on gestures and vocalizations. One of the ways I hear adults disparage gun play is to say that children are *just* swinging their fists or pointing their finger and saying "Bang." Yet this play can involve a complex use of gestures and vocalizations. Gestures can include how to hold one's body to imitate actions such as flying, fighting, or taking power stances. Vocalizations can include using the correct sound to imitate a particular weapon or action.

Even the book *The War Play Dilemma: What Every Parent and Teacher Needs to Know* (Levin and Carlsson-Paige 2004), which has an appreciation for gun play as a way for some children to try to make sense of the world, at times misses the nuance in the nonverbal portion of the play. For example, at one point the authors refer to two children pretending to be Power Rangers. They compare this play to another play scenario, saying it uses "less creativity, imagination, or skills" (64), considering only the fact that the children's ideas came from the TV show and not addressing the physical creativity involved in pursuing the play idea. I think they may not have noticed what was happening behind the TV-character play with the children's unique gestures and vocalizations.

In my experience, children show their creativity in superhero play in their movements and their interactions rather than in storyline or phrasing. Children's movements become more fluid and synchronized with other players as they repeat scenarios. I used to simply label this as "play fighting" and ignore the increasingly complex nonverbal communication that often accompanies this play. Looking back on my early career, I realize that I didn't see the learning happening right in front of me either. I can't help thinking how much less stressed I would have been if I hadn't spent all that time telling children to stop playing guns. I could have stepped back and appreciated the focus and persistence they were demonstrating. As I said earlier, we see what we look for.

In her book, *Se krigsleken - kraft rörelse och förvandling* (2023, currently only available in Swedish), Ebba Theorell explores gun play through a lens of movement and dance. In her research for the book, Theorell found that children show a complexity in their play that is often overlooked when judged as storytelling alone (Ebba Theorell, pers. comm., July 21, 2024).

a barrier to them pretending together, find ways to bridge those differences: "Murphy has never been on a plane. Can you tell her what it's like?" "Amy can't run to the fire, but she was telling me that she could carry fire hoses on her wheelchair."

Your choice of materials, including furniture and props, can give children multiple entry points into the world of imagination. The power of open-ended materials, whether furniture, props, or costumes, resides in the boundless ways children imagine how to use them. Open-ended materials are going to offer the most entry points since each child can bring to mind what a particular prop is in the context of the play. When I started teaching, my preschool classroom had a toy stove, sink, and refrigerator with plastic replicas of food, pots and pans, and dishes. This arrangement is not unique, and you will probably find these same three pieces of furniture represented in most child care programs in the United States (either as three separate pieces or a hybrid unit with all three). In almost every environment I worked in, these pieces had physical details such as plastic burners and knobs for the stove that made it clear what it was supposed to be. Of course, children still pretended the stove was controls for a spaceship, a washing machine, or other things, but compared to the play with other objects and props, this particular play was somewhat limited.

The more details a toy stove has, the less likely a child will use it for anything but a stove. For example, if it has raised burners, it becomes more difficult to pretend it is anything but a stove. Rather than providing a piece of furniture with a very specific purpose like a play stove, you could use an existing shelf or cabinet by simply adding some knobs or taping on a drawing of stove burners or dials to match children's current interests. Children could even make their own drawings to add these details. Then next week it can be revamped into a spaceship or a factory assembly line or anything the children can imagine.

You can also use open-ended materials for props. I often offered playdough, pine cones, bottle caps, and corks for toy food. I have found that children use these materials in ways they do not with the plastic replicas of food that are more typical in early childhood programs. The children could make the dough any shape. They could peel apart the pine cones and mix them with the playdough. Bottle caps and corks could be poured from box to box. The playdough had to be replaced more often, but that provided an opportunity for children to make it every week (see chapter five for ways children can be involved in caring for materials). I have found that shiny or translucent objects such as gold coins, Mardi Gras necklaces, and glass beads inspire magical play. I even introduced some open-ended costumes, large rectangular scarves with Velcro in the corners. Children could wear them like capes, skirts, or strapless dresses. They also used them to wrap dolls and even wrap presents.

In addition to open-ended items, real props can inspire pretend play. Using real pots, dishes, and food packaging gives children a sense of power because they associate these with adults. You can also repurpose kitchen gadgets such as blenders, rice cookers, drying racks, and so forth. You can cut the cord on any electric gadget and remove any sharp blades. You can also use other items associated with grown-ups, such as computer keyboards, phones, and the like. I know of a classroom at a center that mostly serves Mennonite children where the favorite prop is a saddle mounted on a stool because only grown-ups and older children ride horses. In my own classroom, a French press and, later, a Keurig single-use coffee maker were favorites.

When I worked in Brooklyn, New York, I was struck by how many children were interested in washers and dryers. I had only taught in Minnesota, where parents often went to the basement to do laundry. But in Brooklyn, most children had weekly trips to the laundromat where they helped their families do laundry. Many of them helped load and unload the machines. I finally put two empty boxes with doors cut in them and filled them with clothes, and added a small hamper in the room. One child in particular played laundromat repeatedly with these. But I soon saw other children use the boxes as a microwave, a cabinet, a magic box, and a hiding spot. The hamper was a turtle shell or a cage when turned upside down. The possibilities seemed endless.

There is still a place for toys to be used in pretend play. Costumes such as uniforms, fancy dresses, and capes that are sized for children can inspire a wide range of power play. Some real items are too expensive, heavy, or dangerous to use the real thing, such as power tools and medical equipment.

Overall, the goal is to inspire imagination, so take notice of which materials inspire children the most. It will vary depending on children's lived experience, interests, and abilities. Here are some ideas for imaginative materials that support children's agency:

OPEN-ENDED MATERIALS

- Boxes
- Big paper and tape to roll it into tubes (demonstrate this if the children need guidance)
- Playdough
- Pine cones
- Scarves

REAL ITEMS

- Dishes and utensils
- Pots and pans
- Dish racks
- Cutting boards
- Phones and tablets (or phone/tablet cases)
- Keyboards

PURCHASED REPLICA ITEMS

- Fire helmets
- Toy tools
- Doctor kits
- Steering wheels
- Cash registers
- Capes
- Community helper uniforms
- Dresses, skirts, tutus (see chapter three for more discussion about dress-up)

Self-Efficacy

Imagination allows children to feel successful in their endeavors, which can positively affect their self-efficacy. They can enter play in a way that matches their skill level. The multiple entry points let children who want to follow the lead of others have roles while others can direct play. Children can choose physically active roles or more stationary ones. The fantasy element allows children who may not know the particular scenario to add a role outside the narrative.

For children who need support entering play, the adult can help the child match their skills and interests with the various potential roles. Some children may simply not know how to enter play. I often see children stop peers from playing to ask if they can play. The peers often say no because, from their perspective, the child interrupted their play. The adult can help a child enter play seamlessly by helping them in two ways: the child needs to know the particular play scenario and also determine which roles are suitable to their interest or skill level. When I see a child either watching or trying to join and being rebuffed, I usually approach and say, "Let's see if we can figure out what they're playing. I think I heard Frank say something about Black Panther. Do you know who that is? I think he rescues people. Should we have him rescue us?" Sometimes a child chooses a role without finding out what the others are playing. Other times the play is based on a movie they don't know. At times a child will choose a role that involves more decision-making or negotiation than they are capable of.

Because many pretend play scenarios have roles for different skill levels, this play offers a chance for expert players to mentor others (that is, exercise power *for* them). If Akari plays the baby every day, she not only enjoys the play but can also watch what Zehra does when she is the mom. Perhaps Akari will eventually play the big sister or maybe even mom using some of what she learned from Zehra. In the meantime, she enjoys the role she is playing. The group nature of the play allows for smaller steps in acquiring skills while still participating.

Self-Regulation

As I mentioned, children often enter a flow state during pretend play that also allows them to practice the executive function skills needed for self-regulation. Adults can foster this learning by giving children time and space to imagine and intervening when there is a conflict or a child gets upset. Usually conflict and upset are the result of a gap in executive function skills. Knowing that these skills are developing can help an adult approach situations with understanding. Here is a summary of some of those skills and how they relate to imagination and pretend play:

IMPULSE CONTROL (INHIBITORY CONTROL)

- A child can only act and speak in ways that are appropriate for the role they are inhabiting.
- Children have to refrain from aggression when disagreeing with peers' ideas for the pretend play scenario.

FOCUS (INHIBITORY CONTROL)

- A child pays attention to what the other players are saying or doing while ignoring the voices of others who are not playing.
- A child is able to ignore the strange feeling of dress-up costumes or props that might feel different from their usual clothing.
- A child focuses on the play scenario and characters for long periods of time when entering flow state.

THINKING THROUGH POSSIBLE IDEAS (MENTAL FLEXIBILITY)

- A child takes into account both their mental imagery and the actual environment.
- A child can change roles during play.
- A child can think of potential scenarios that other players may also like.
- A child can use an object to represent a different object.

DEALING WITH CHANGE (MENTAL FLEXIBILITY)

- A child can step in and out of the imaginary realm when needed.
- Other children can change their roles during play.
- Other children can change the scenario during play.

WORKING MEMORY

- A child can step into and out of the role as needed without losing the thread of the pretend play.
- A child must keep track of multiple roles and props.

REGULATION

- A child can experience a range of emotions (even if mimicked) while staying regulated.
- Children are highly motivated to keep playing so they are more likely to resolve conflicts or emotional setbacks.
- Children enter a flow state so they may play longer.

Connection

Imagination happens inside a person's mind. No one else can see what they see in their mental imagery. And yet the embodied nature of pretending allows others to get a glimpse of what is going on in the other person's mind. Pretending together is one of the main ways children make connections and build friendships. It becomes their shared dialogue in the way that adults might have in-depth conversations.

Adults can also strengthen relationships with children by pretending with them. The important thing is to follow the child's lead. You can add small details to the play but let them make most of the choices. It's easy to take over in play as an adult, forgetting how much mental flexibility it takes to pretend. I remember a time when three children were playing restaurant. I joined them, and before I realized it I told a story of going to a restaurant and looking at the menu. I brought over paper and asked what food we could put on the menu. Luckily, they were not deterred by my overzealous participation. Paul, the leader of the play, stood at the counter (a toy stove) and turned to one of the others and said, "Welcome to McDonald's. What would you like?"

Following children's lead allows them to use their own experience and prior knowledge to create the situation for the play. I have found it helpful to ask a child about their experiences when they are trying to join others who are already playing. For example, if a child had never been to a fast-food place where orders are taken at a counter, they wouldn't know what to visualize when Paul asked for their order. They wouldn't need experience at the specific restaurant but rather any restaurant that has counter service. What each child mentally pictures, smells, or tastes may differ but there would be enough commonality and connection to keep the playing going. Shared experiences lead to shared narratives.

Adults from a child's family, community, and group care all add to that child's mental library of stories and situations. Real-life experiences are often replayed by preschoolers. Children also reenact narratives from books, stories, movies, and other shows. Adults in group care have a rich opportunity to introduce children to books and stories. When a child asks you to read a book again, the child gains new understanding each time. With each reading, children's mental imagery grows until they are immersed in the world of the book. It becomes more than just a book. One of my childhood memories is staring at a page of the book *Where the Wild Things Are* by Maurice Sendak. My mom had read it to me countless times. I would look at the image of Max's room when a forest is growing, and I could *see* the trees taking over the furniture and imagined them soon taking over my own room. The familiarity of the book, both the story and the pictures, allowed me to feel like I was in the book too. Or, more accurately, I felt like my world and the world of the book had merged.

Storytelling is another wonderful way to spark mental imagery. The absence of illustrations means children fill in the details with their mental imagery. You can encourage this by including multiple senses in your story. If you retell "Three Billy Goats Gruff," what does the sunshine feel like? What does the troll's breath smell like? You can make up your own stories, but you can also retell stories. I have found fairy tales a great place to start. Stephanie Goloway, author of *Happily Ever Resilient: Using Fairy Tales to Nurture Children through Adversity*, describes fairy tales as being pared down to the basic story structure and generic stock characters. Children can identify with them at so many levels because they are open-ended rather than specific (Bernt-Santy and Goloway 2024). Fairy tales are similar to young children's pretend play in which certain characters are good and others are bad, with little nuance. Bad characters simply die off or disappear without the real-life consequences we adults consider. Fairy tales offer children a common framework to play collaboratively even if they have diverse lived experiences.

You can simply retell the story as you remember it, or you can adapt it. One of the favorite stories I tell was based on "The Emperor's New Clothes." In my version, it's a teacher instead of an emperor. He is "the nicest, smartest, best teacher in the whole world." Of course, he actually rivals Cinderella's stepmother, making the children watch while he plays with all the toys and then making the children clean up while he watches. It is basic power reversal. But then a mysterious tailor makes clothes that only the nicest, smartest, best people can see. When the teacher realizes he's been tricked, he runs off, leaving the children to run the classroom.

Storytelling and book reading can connect a group of children by giving them common experiences to facilitate collaborative pretend play. It gives them more entry points. Of course, they will find many ways to play together beyond the stories you introduce. The most important things are allowing time and space to explore together, providing props to inspire play, and building bridges for children struggling to join.

———————————————————

Preschoolers engage in imaginative play more than any other age group because they can separate their mental imagery from their perception of the real world; they feel comfortable in sliding back and forth between the two. They do this not simply in their mind but with their whole body. This embodiment of their mental imagery enables children to enter a flow state during play, allowing them to experience a wide range of situations and emotions that would not be possible in real life. They make sense of the outer world and match it with their inner world. Pretend play is the embodiment of this inner world. It gives others a window into who we are. It also gives us a window to our own understanding of who we are.

CHAPTER THREE

Identity

"I'm getting ready for Seder." Noa, a four-year-old who is Jewish, is putting two large scarves on the table for a tablecloth. Then she sets out the plates and cups. She sets a plate and cup in the middle of the table and tells me, "This is Elijah's cup." George, a child who is not Jewish, sits at the table. Noa sings the song "Dayenu." Then she passes a plate of cardboard rectangles and tells George to take some matzah. George does not know what matzah is, but he understands that they are playing dinner. He takes one of the rectangles and pretends to eat it.

Earlier I described children's imagination as boundless. But children have limits to what they play. Noa acted out a Seder that mimicked elements of Seders she has been part of. George participated, but he was limited in how he did so. He had experience eating dinner, but he did not join in the singing of "Dayenu." In this case the limit is due to lack of experience. Additionally, as they develop their multiple cultural identities, children may view some roles or scenarios as unsuitable for themselves and impose boundaries on their play or imagination.

For example, a girl may pretend to be a dragon, but she will announce that she is a girl dragon. She can imagine being a dragon but not a boy.

Noa following the cultural dictates of Seder and the dragon girl announcing her character's gender are both examples of children's imagination being bound by their cultural identity. Culture is the values, behaviors, and ways of understanding that a group of people share. Each person has several cultural identities based on race, ethnicity, place of birth, gender, family structure, economic class, and similar characteristics (Derman-Sparks and Edwards 2020). Children first develop their cultural identities based on experiences from their family life, but they don't think of this as culture. As David Foster Wallace (2009) reminds us in his 2005 commencement speech at Kenyon College, culture is like the water fish swim in: it's everywhere but you don't notice it until you are taken out of it. Children experience culture as just the way things are—at least they do until they meet others with different experiences; it's simply the way you do things. Thus, children develop behaviors based on their understanding of themselves and those around them. But children don't do this uniformly, and identity development is not a linear process. They will occasionally veer outside of these boundaries they impose.

I find the model of cultural schema to be helpful when appreciating children's play boundaries. A schema is a mental framework that a person creates to allow shortcuts (also called heuristics) when thinking about something. These shortcuts include scripts about how to behave as well as what to expect from others in different social contexts. I find it helpful to think of a schema as a mental map. I recently created a mental map in the literal sense when I moved to a new neighborhood.

When I moved to the west side of St. Paul last year, I knew two main streets to go east/west to get to the three bridges that brought me to downtown. The first few weeks I had to focus to make sure I turned at the right places. A month in, I was able to follow my route automatically so I could think about other things while driving. But then a few months later, construction blocked my usual commute. Suddenly I couldn't rely on automatic cognition. Again, I learned a new route. At the same time, when I wasn't in a hurry, I would take other streets. Some ended at parks or railroad tracks or curved to take me out of my way. Other times, I would find a shortcut or a route with a nice view of the river. I also used my phone's map to discover a quick way to a highway that allowed me to bypass rush hour traffic. My mental map started with some rudimentary routes. Over time my mental map became more complex, and it allowed for variation.

I use this analogy to illustrate several salient points about my schema:

- It starts simply and becomes more complex.
- It does not happen in a linear fashion.
- It evolves over time.
- I tried routes that were not part of my mental map.
  - This did not negate my map but rather added to it.

- I had multiple routes to use depending on the situation.
- As this mental map solidified, I relied more on automatic cognition.
  - I followed routes without thinking consciously.

In terms of cultural schema, I have observed children following a similar process:

- It starts simply and becomes more complex.
- It does not happen in a linear fashion.
- It evolves over time.
- Children sometimes act in ways that contradict their stated ideas about gender or other cultural norms.
  - These nonstereotypical behaviors do not negate stereotypes they hold.

- Children act in a variety of ways depending on the situation.
- As their schema solidifies, they rely more on automatic cognition.
  - They act more without thinking consciously about cultural identities (which is to say their implicit bias is building).

Cultural Identity and Power

Cultural identity affects everything a child does. The biggest impact it has on pretend play is the scripts that children use for their play. Noa's experience with Seder gave her a script. In this case, I am using the term *script* in both the theatrical sense of behaviors, actions, and words that are appropriate for a particular play scenario and in the social psychology sense as it applies to real-life situations. Children can only use the scripts they have encountered in their lived experience. These scripts are not exact replicas of experiences but rather contain elements of experiences. For example, a child might make up a monster that has wings like a bird and a tail like a lion—its elements are pulled from real life. Even in Noa's case, she is acting out Seder based on her perception, so she focuses on the plate and cup and the song she sang. At next year's Seder, she will have a better understanding of what she does during the meal, so she may start to notice what adults or older children are doing. At that point, she may take on the role of an adult when she plays Seder. Acting out a lived experience reinforces the scripts children follow, and they can become more detailed over time.

As children develop their cultural identity, it affects all four elements of power: agency, self-efficacy, self-regulation, and connection. Children ideally develop a sense of belonging within their cultural groups. Part of feeling like you belong is feeling that your presence matters to others, that your actions affect others. Simply put, it increases your sense of agency. As we will see, the way a child's cultural identity is affirmed, or not affirmed, affects their self-efficacy. Healthy cultural identity requires self-regulation, especially regarding how an individual interacts with others from differing cultures. Of course, a child's cultural identity can help them connect to others who share their identity. Perhaps it's not as obvious that healthy cultural identity can also help children connect to those from other cultural groups. Pretending has a vital role in cultural identity development, and adults can help make this a healthy experience.

Agency

Over time, children increase in the number of scripts they act out. Many of these scripts come from their own lived experience and the stories they hear, both of which are related to the cultural context they are raised in. I noticed how context affects children's play recently when I started a new job.

We set up a few computer keyboards that we brought in to use as props. At my last center, children often used the keyboards to pretend to be working. Many of the parents worked white-collar jobs, often doing some of the work at home, so children saw them clicking away on a computer. But the culture of the children's families at this center was very different. Most parents did not use a laptop at home. They used their phones, which is exactly what the children usually pretended when taking on a parent role. They would scroll their social media, look up information, and take pictures. The children only used keyboards when they played doctor.

These scripts help form children's cultural schema as they learn to use certain behaviors, actions, and words in various situations. These actions match those used by others who share their cultural identity, creating a sense of an in-group. Your in-group includes the people who share your cultural actions, beliefs, and understanding. Forming that sense of one's in-group is a natural part of development, and it is important because it gives children a sense of belonging. This sense of belonging to an in-group correlates to the feeling of having an impact on the world, in other words, a sense of agency (Li et al. 2019). Fitting into in-groups does mean that children also notice those who belong to out-groups, those the child does not belong to. Children also develop scripts for out-groups, but these scripts tend to be more generalized since children don't share that lived experience.

Scripts for in-groups and out-groups can be useful because they allow us to fill in missing information so we can make decisions and act. I can't possibly know everything about a person, but I may make assumptions based on what I know about them culturally. If I give directions to someone in St. Paul, I will probably give them driving directions, assuming they have a car. When I lived in New York City, I would have given directions for the subway. If my assumption is wrong, I can correct myself, but I choose a script based on my initial understanding.

Because these scripts are shortcuts, they can result in the formation of stereotypes, especially for out-groups. The collaborative nature of pretend play can be helpful in avoiding the pitfalls of stereotyping. Just as the pretend play allows one child to reinforce their understanding of their in-group, another child can gain more understanding of an out-group. George learned that a Seder is a ritual Noa's family participates in. He may not know specific details, but he is learning that what is a religious out-group for him also has holidays and rituals. This may help George approach people from his out-groups with curiosity rather than making sweeping assumptions.

Pretend play won't always revolve around holidays, of course. There are many other ways that culture shows up in play. Differences in sleep practices may show up in family play, for example. The adult can help bridge cultural differences. If there are disagreements among children, the adult can start by saying, "Different families do things differently. Where does your family sleep?" Once you ask each child, then restate their answers. "Isn't that interesting? Each person in your family has their own room and his family members all sleep in one room. How are you going to sleep in your game?" Simple statements about difference demonstrate an acceptance of diversity and facilitate the continuation of pretend play.

Self-efficacy

For children to grow their sense of self-efficacy, they must receive affirmation of their developing cultural identity. All children need this, but children who share a culture with a majority of others in a group care setting often have this affirmed regularly. Other children may not have their culture affirmed as often. A child who joins group care only to realize that the way they eat at home is considered weird or impolite by the other children or adults might not only feel stressed but also worry something is fundamentally wrong with them or their family. Feeling part of a group contributes to self-esteem and can positively affect self-efficacy. Feeling you don't belong has the opposite effect.

A child's cultural scripts may influence the play scenario, for example, defining what "going to work" means in play. One example that has come up repeatedly over the twenty years I have been training on gun play is children from families of hunters or those with a parent who is a police officer or serves in the armed forces. What effect does banning gun play have on a child whose mom carries a firearm for work? Does that child feel like their family is welcome in that program?

Adults make assumptions based on our own experiences, just as children do. When we reflect on our own cultural identities, it helps ensure we approach differences with curiosity. Otherwise, we can inadvertently assume that the way we do things is the correct way and other ways are simply failed attempts at acting like us. For example, it is easy to think someone

Do not leave the children who don't share the majority culture of the room responsible for teaching the others. You—as the adult—can help give children information. You can involve families in this process by approaching every family with curiosity about their family life. You can also complement this with books and storytelling. Use multiple books to represent a culture, because each member of a culture has a unique experience, so a variety of stories are needed. When reading books that might be windows or sliding glass doors for children, be sure to talk about both similarities and differences their families might have with those in the books.

Here are other ways you can counteract stereotyping out-groups:

LEARN FROM FAMILIES

- Who are the important people in the child's life?
- What are their dreams for their child?
- What does the child like to do at home?

SEEK FAMILY INPUT FOR THE PRETEND PLAY AREA SO PROPS REFLECT HOME LIFE

- Ask for packaging from food.
- Ask about implements or dishes used at mealtimes.
- Ask about the decorations in the home.

ASK FAMILY MEMBERS TO COME IN AND TELL A STORY ABOUT THEIR FAMILY

- It does not have to be culturally specific.
- It could be a story from a family member's childhood.

READ BOOKS THAT PROVIDE MIRRORS, WINDOWS, AND SLIDING GLASS DOORS FOR CHILDREN (SEE P. 35)

- Mirrors reflect some of the children's experiences.
- Windows give a glimpse into experiences of others.
- Sliding glass doors tell stories such that a child can immerse themselves in a world that differs from their own experience.

ENCOURAGE COLLABORATIVE PRETEND PLAY

- One child's script can serve as a window for another child.
- Adults can bridge knowledge gaps between children.

speaks with an accent, forgetting that we all have an accent. If most of those around you speak with the same accent as you, you might think that you don't have an accent at all. The same is true for most things in our life: what food you eat for breakfast, how you deal with conflict, what it means to be on time, and so on. Fostering an environment that addresses our bias is key to supporting children's self-efficacy.

Self-reflection helps us examine our implicit bias, the assumptions we make without even realizing it. We are all capable of implicit bias. These biases come from the mental shortcuts that we developed in our own childhoods, and recent research has demonstrated how this implicit bias plays out in early childhood environments. For example, Walter Gilliam and several others conducted research that found that adults working with young children watch Black boys more closely than others for signs of misbehavior (Gilliam et al. 2016). If we are not careful, we may interpret a Black boy engaging in power over play as misbehavior rather than simply play. I have found that self-talk in the moment helps me. Before I intervene, I mentally step back to see if anyone is actually in danger. Then I look to see if other children are playing in a similar way, and ask, "Am I only noticing this in some of the children?" While the answer may be uncomfortable at times, it is better than following through on my initial impulse to intervene based on my implicit bias.

Of course, those of us working with young children are not the only ones with bias. US society as a whole is biased, especially in relation to race. Black boys are policed to an extent that other children are not. My own experience is in line with research showing that adults expel Black boys at a much higher rate than other children (Zimmerman 2024). Age-appropriate behaviors are seen by many adults as challenging when they are done by Black boys, especially if the child is bigger than average (Gilliam et al. 2016). Black boys have been murdered because they had toy guns (Zola 2017). Knowing this, we adults working with young children can give Black children space and time to engage in power play in the spaces we control and hold safe for them. We also need to communicate with families to find out how we can best support their children to stay safe in the broader world. We can work with families to let children know where they can engage in gun play and where it might not be safe to play this way (Kisa Marx, pers. comm., June 23, 2024). As a white educator, I felt awkward having these conversations at first, but I have found Black families receptive. I can't pretend that my experience is the same as the Black children in my care. All families need to be reassured that power play is typical, while at the same time, different families will need to be supported in different ways.

Addressing cultural bias is essential for children's self-efficacy. Children should view prejudice based on their identity as a problem with the perpetrator, not a problem with the child or their identity. Self-efficacy relies on each child feeling good about who they are.

Self-regulation

Healthy identity development in conjunction with regulation skills can lead to healthy social connections. A child's cultural development leads to mental shortcuts that can result in implicit bias, and a lack of regulation skills can mean that these biases take over. If Julie, a nondisabled child, grows up thinking wheelchair users are unable to do things without adult help, she may walk right past Ian, who uses a wheelchair, to ask another child to join her in play. Julie is not intentionally excluding Ian, but rather her implicit bias—her mental heuristic (or shortcut)—causes her not to see Ian as a potential playmate.

Inhibitory control can counter these implicit biases. In this case, Julie could pause before walking past Ian. After pausing, Julie could consciously change her focus, looking again at people she may not have noticed when she first looked around. Including Ian may also involve mental flexibility. If Julie was going to play Jasmine and was looking for someone to be Aladdin and fly on a magic carpet, she may have pictured someone she would run with. She would have to picture a different way of moving to mimic flying. These are fairly advanced skills, and this mental flexibility is unlikely to happen in the preschool years without an adult helping. The adult could tell Julie, "I know Ian likes Aladdin. Let's go ask him," and then say to both Julie and Ian, "Julie wants to fly on a magic carpet. I wonder how you two could pretend to fly?"

This is more effective if the adults proactively and continually bridge children's play so playing with someone with different abilities than yourself is the norm.

Lettie, a paraplegic child with limited speech, had recently started at a center. On her third day, she was on the playground with her paraprofessional, Keala. Nearby, a few children were playing sharks and minnows. Keala noticed Lettie watching the others and asked, "Should we be minnows too?" Lettie smiled and pointed, and they were off. After they were chased for a few minutes, Justin said, "I'm tired of being the shark. Can you be the shark, Keala?" Keala replied, "I'm just here to help Lettie move around, you'll have to see if she wants to be the shark." Justin asked Lettie and she smiled. Keala explained, "When she smiles like that, she's saying yes." And they were off again. Back inside, Justin brought over a French press and mugs, asking Lettie, "Do you want to play coffee shop?" She smiled and he set the items on her tray and said, "Can I have hot chocolate?" Lettie pushed the mugs around. Justin picked up the mug and pretended to drink.

Children at this center were used to being in a class with children of varying abilities, but Lettie was the first child the others had met who needed a full-time paraprofessional. The first day, it was apparent that children weren't sure how to interpret Lettie's gestures. They greeted her and expressed curiosity but did not treat her as a playmate. After the sharks and minnows game, children would ask Lettie to join them in play. Occasionally, Keala would have to help the others read Lettie's expressions and gestures, but usually the children could do it on their own.

Adults can use strategies from this book to nurture executive function and self-regulation skills. Over time, children will be able to navigate many cultural differences in their play without adult assistance. Fostering these interactions will increase children's sense of power because it increases connections with others.

Connection

Pretend play's collaborative nature connects children to each other. Each player shares a bit of their internal imagery, and, in turn, each player experiences the internal imagery of others, discovering the complexity of their peers' thoughts and ideas. In this way, children expand their understanding that they have a unique perspective that is different from others, during this important life stage when they are first developing their cultural and gender identity. As children are developing their cultural schema based on their understanding of their in-groups, they can be susceptible to generalizing about those in other groups. Children notice differences among individuals from their own in-group, but they are less likely to notice variation in other groups. Other groups can seem to be a monolith because children typically notice how a group differs from them. Collaborative pretend play counters this tendency to stereotyping.

Our main role as adults is to provide the time and space for this play. Having a variety of props and materials invites many types of play and multiple entry points. Children can find ways to play with others who differ from them and connect with a wider variety of children. These differences may relate to race, ethnicity, and many other cultural identities. However, when children engage in power play, gender may be the most salient.

The Case Study of Q and A

To illustrate how a child's developing cultural identity influences what they choose to pretend and how they play with power, I will take a closer look at one specific child. I will also focus on one specific element of cultural identity, gender identity, to allow for some simplicity in an admittedly complicated process. The child's experiences are unique, but the way personal and cultural identity play out for Q shines a light on how cultural identity and imaginative play influence each other.

Q was a preschooler in my classroom over a decade before I wrote this book. Throughout the years, I have told stories about them in my public speaking to illustrate the creativity of young children. The story of Princess Leia and Queen Amidala that opened chapter two is one of the most memorable stories for me. I reconnected with Q while writing this book. They were seventeen when I interviewed them. When they were in my classroom they were being raised as a girl and they were assigned female at birth. In their teen years, they came out as nonbinary, meaning they do not neatly fit into either category of boy or girl. Q uses they/them pronouns. As an outlier of cultural norms around gender identity, Q has been very reflective around the topic of gender.

After interviewing Q, I also interviewed their mom and twenty-year-old sister to get a broader picture of their play and development. Mom is cisgender and A is transgender. The two siblings asked to be identified as Q and A in a nod to both a Star Trek character and the question-and-answer format of the interview. Mom agreed to simply be identified as Mom. Dad is mentioned but I was unable to interview him due to logistics.

In this case study, we focused on Q's play in two main places: home and my classroom. I want to set the scene of what my classroom looked like at the time. I set the conditions that allowed for the variety of play happening in the classroom. Here is my memory of that time:

Pretend play took up most of my classroom. There was a nook with a child-sized couch and a countertop with computer keyboards. Just outside the nook on one side was a toy stove, refrigerator, and sink. The other side had a dresser of costumes. Next to the dresser was a loft. There were more hooks on the wall for the bigger costumes, mostly quinceañera dresses, bags and purses, and superhero capes. This offered three distinct spaces for pretending: upstairs in the loft, downstairs with the kitchen appliances, and nearby in the nook.

There were three children, Sarah, Jacinda, and Q, who played princess most days. They also played family with a larger group of children. Josh and Patrick typically pretended in a more physical way, playing out themes such as Spider-Man or Star Wars. Q at times would join Josh and Patrick when they were battling. Q played a wide variety of roles in any play theme. When playing family, Q might be the baby, the cat, the mom, or the dad. Even when they played mom, Q had a way of bringing unique scenarios. I can recall one time when Q sat at the top of the loft stairs banging on a drum, yelling, "Kids, you must go to bed now! You need to go upstairs to bed when I finish banging my drum!"

The term *cisgender* or *cis* describes a person whose gender identity matches their sex assigned at birth. The term *transgender* or *trans* describes a person whose gender identity does *not* match their sex assigned at birth. They could be a trans woman, a trans man, or a nonbinary person. *Nonbinary* means that the person does not identify as a man or a woman.

Every major medical and psychological organization advises that children and teens be supported if they identify as trans (or simply express their gender in non-normative ways). Data shows that rates of depression and suicide diminish as the self-esteem and sense of agency of these children increases (Edwards 2025).

Research shows that the belief that there are only two genders that correspond with two biological sexes is mistaken. Rather, multiple chromosomal combinations and hormone levels are associated with biological sex (Purves et al. 2001). When a person's gender is reaffirmed by their family and community, even if that gender identity contradicts the typical alignment with their biological sex, their health outcomes improve (James et al. 2022).

Banging on a drum was not the typical bedtime routine at home, of course—Q was simply exaggerating the role of a parent. The play was based on experience while still being imaginative. In reality, Q recalls that their mom and dad told different bedtime stories: "Mom would tell her version of classic fairy tales. I don't think she was that into them. But she would always make the female characters more empowered than some versions of the stories. Q's sister A remembers Mom's stories were always about the "freedom to be who you are." Mom confirms this, saying, "I know I emphasized the agency of the girl characters. I don't remember telling fairy tales but I'm sure I retold stories from books."

Meanwhile, Dad's stories came from a different literary universe. As Q remembers, "Dad would tell me and my sister stories that were his own made-up stories based on the Star Wars universe. He didn't retell the stories from the movies. He made up stories we would enjoy. One was about Luke needing to use the bathroom on the Death Star."

Mom's and Dad's stories conveyed both cultural values and a cast of fictional characters and worlds for Q to act out in their play. Q also learned characters from other children when they entered group care. Here is how they remember their time in my preschool classroom:

I played a lot of different roles: family, princess, Star Wars, fairies, and cats. I played princess a lot but mostly because Sarah and Jacinda always played princess and that's who I liked to play with. We also played family. Sometimes I was the sister. One time I was a cat that threw up. We thought it was the funniest thing. I guess it was my way of being the one in charge of the play. I had the power, I guess.

Another time, we wanted a dad in the game but it was just the three of us [Sarah, Jacinda, and Q]. They asked me to be the dad so I did. It wasn't a big deal for me to play boy characters. But thinking back, I guess they never did. But for me, it didn't really matter. The joy wasn't in the gender, it was in the playing.

At home Q pretended with A. Being three years older, A didn't have a lot of shared interests with Q. The two generally only played together when pretending. Q's interest in princess play aligned with A's interest in knights. Here is how A describes it:

I remember being very interested in playing knights and castle. Q was interested in playing princess. We had cardboard blocks at home that had castle features printed on them. We often built castles to use in our pretend play. Most of our play interests were so diametrically opposed that we had to find entry points in our play. Princess and knight became our "shared dialogue." We also could play Star Wars because it also allowed princesses and warriors and, frequently, "warrior princesses." A few years later [when Q was in kindergarten or first grade], we started watching [the TV show] *Xena: Warrior Princess* with our dad and incorporated that into our play.

Q and I are both chronic daydreamers, always watching movies in our heads. Pretending with Q was a chance for me to get a glimpse of what was in their head. It created an empathetic connection between us. When I was about nine or ten, I was pretending less. I found I was playing less with Q. A few years later, Q started playing Dungeons and Dragons (D&D) with me and our dad. We played every week. Playing D&D is just kids on the playground but with dice. Q and I started connecting again like we did when we pretended.

The cultural transmission of stories and values from parent to child is not simply filling a child's mind with ideas. The child plays an active part in the process, reacting to their experiences and fitting them into their own understanding of self. In Q's case, Mom was quite uncomfortable with how much they played princess. She actually came to me with these concerns. Here is what she remembers:

I was very uncomfortable with Q's interest in princess play. I didn't want them learning to equate femininity with being passive. I was influenced by the writing of Bruno Bettelheim, so I was accepting of gun play and other violent-themed play. Children were attracted to it to experience power. I was fine with A playing knight and making swords out of everything. I came to you to ask how I get Q to stop playing princess all the time. You asked me if I would be worried if they were playing guns. And I realized I wouldn't. This was just about power.

I honestly don't remember the exact conversation, but her recollection makes me realize that this was a new concept for me. Q was a catalyst for the ideas in this book, and this case study is me coming full circle some thirteen years later. As I have stated, Q's play has stuck with me because it highlighted much of what I have observed about power play over the years.

In my interviews, I also got to learn more about the play that happened after Q left my classroom. In some ways, everything matches the person I knew, but there was little that I would have predicted at the time. I include some of this here to show how it related to later experiences. Here is Q's summary of their tween and teen years:

> I got involved in theater in middle school. When I was thirteen, I realized I started my gender journey. I was trying to figure out what made sense for me. I finally came out as nonbinary. Right after I came out, I refused to take any female roles in the plays I was in. Outside of theater, I wouldn't dress in anything feminine. This year, I realized I don't really care. It's not a big deal for me to dress more masculine or more feminine. And now I can play roles regardless of gender.

Q's comments about the last few years were surprisingly similar to their attitudes in preschool, especially around pretending or, in this case, acting. Their journey to this understanding of their own identity did not seem to be a straight path, but ultimately where they arrived is not far off from the person I remember. Their sister A remembers some other points that involved imagination:

> We were playing D&D regularly. I think both of us explored our gender identity at times during this play. I remember one campaign [an ongoing storyline that happens over multiple sessions] where Q was a character named Mary. In the middle of the campaign, Q quit. Not long after, Q told us they were nonbinary.
>
> I remember creating a female character for myself for one of our campaigns [A was living as a boy up until this point]. I was somewhat aware of what I was doing. I was wondering if I was a girl. This was a way to see how it felt. It wasn't a clean break from living as a boy to living as a girl, it was a chance for me to explore.

Of course, pretending to be something does not make a person change. But it is a way to outwardly embody one's internal feelings. The story of Q and A makes it clear that this is not a simple or one-way process. It isn't "I am a girl therefore I play princess," nor is it "if I am a boy and I play princess, my identity might change." One child may feel like wearing a flowy dress because of the way it will move as they spin. Another child may want to wear a dress because it is associated with femininity and being a girl in their developing gender schema. We only see the outside expression. We don't know what the child is feeling internally. What we can do is affirm that children have agency in their play and exploration by providing them space, time, and materials. Our role is not to change what the child feels inside but to give them freedom to outwardly express those feelings.

Gender Schema and Gender Norms

Just like cultural schema in general, gender schemas allow people to fill in incomplete information. In my experience, when I go into a group care setting, children and adults generally assume either that I am someone's father or that I am there to repair something. Unless I am expected, it is rare that someone assumes that I am an educator. All of us make assumptions in similar ways, and it would be overwhelming if we never relied on these shortcuts. It only becomes problematic when we fail to realize we might make incorrect assumptions.

My friend Tiago visited my classroom. We had been visiting a neighborhood laundromat and the children were interested in how a washing machine worked. Tiago was a maintenance technician. I asked Tiago to show the children how he tests a washing machine using one at the center.

When he entered the classroom, he was wearing jeans and a T-shirt. He had long hair and a long beard. Jarrod and Claudia ran up to him. Tiago smiled and Jarrod lightly punched him on the arm. Tiago laughed and Claudia jumped up and grabbed him. Tiago laughed again and said, "Hey there. I'm Tiago."

We had other guests come to our program that year, but Tiago was the first man. Relying on their gender schema, Jarrod and Claudia made assumptions about how to interact with Tiago. They saw his clothing and beard and assumed he was male. They both had experience roughhousing with me and with male relatives. As they ran toward Tiago, he smiled, indicating to them that they had permission to interact with him the way they interacted with other men. When Jarrod punched his arm and Claudia jumped up on him, Tiago's instant reaction was to laugh. He saw their actions as welcoming gestures.

I realize that some readers will read the above vignette and notice that Jarrod and Claudia did not ask permission to act in the way they did with Tiago. Readers who are not men are probably more inclined to feel this way. In this case, Tiago, Jarrod, Claudia, and I all shared a similar superordinate gender schema (see below) that accepts these physical actions as an acceptable way to greet a man. The same children would typically take a step or two toward a woman and say hello, or if they knew the woman as already a friend of mine, they might hug her. This is an example of a cultural script. It is not to say that everyone follows this script. And, of course, there is more nuance to it. If Jarrod was an adult just meeting Tiago, he wouldn't punch his arm. Tiago and I generally hugged when greeting each other, but only after becoming friends. On the other hand, I recognized the level of trust that Jarrod and Claudia showed Tiago by interacting in this way. I go into more detail in chapter four about consent but include this example to show how gender schema affects the scripts we use with others.

Each of us develops two interrelated gender schema, *superordinate* and *own-gender* schema. Superordinate gender schema is the understanding of how gender works in the world. This includes the norms of the child's family and immediate community as well as the societal norms in the larger culture. Own-gender schema is the child's view of their own gender identity.

Superordinate gender schema will vary from family to family. Some of the messages children receive on gender will be explicit; for example, "Girls don't . . ." or "Boys don't . . ." may be spoken directly. In my experience, these messages may come from a family's personal values, cultural beliefs, or religious teachings. Children also pick up on the words, actions, and attitudes that family or community members use. For example, words such as *pretty*, *cute*, *adorable*, and *sweet* are used for girls. Terms usually used for boys include *handsome*, *strong*, *fast*, and *active*. Adults will often apologize if they use one of these terms for the "wrong" gender, such as calling a boy *pretty* or a girl *handsome*.

In addition to the words themselves, there is a difference in the substance of what is described. I have seen adults frequently comment on girls' appearance, both clothes and features. This conveys that looks are important for girls. I have also seen adults frequently comment on boys' strength and speed, giving those attributes an inflated sense of significance. If a child's gender expression does not conform to cultural norms, adults often simply refrain from making comments.

During the COVID-19 pandemic in 2020 and 2021, I would pick up children at the curb and escort them to their classroom. The building had several programs, so we would pass by several adults. Many of the adults would greet us as we walked through the hallways. Some adults got to know children by name or knew something about the child they would comment on, such as, "How is your sister, Eleanor?" But it was striking how girls who had long hair or wore dresses would receive comments such as, "Don't you look pretty!" or "You're so cute!" Girls who had shorter hair or wore a T-shirt and pants would hear, "Good morning!," the same greeting boys would hear. One girl who looked like a child model would receive even more comments about her looks. One of the differences was the tone of voice or added exclamations: "Oh, don't you look *so* pretty!" I have always witnessed this to some degree but I never got to witness half a dozen interactions with one child at a time. How could children not get the message that looks were what gave girls power?

At the same time, this does not mean that girls playing princess will learn that looks are the *only* source of power. I know that I used to think princess play *taught* girls to be passive and reinforced stereotypes about femininity. But I have found that princess play is merely a frame for children to take on any number of scenarios (Burton 2021). Returning to the case study earlier in this chapter, Q played princess frequently, sometimes incorporating themes of a battling warrior princess. Other times the play was focused on dressing as fancy as possible for the ball.

Society's emphasis on strength and speed for boys and male characters in movies and other media often encourages boys to express power through weapon play or superhero play. Children choose their roles from the ones that seem available to them. Many adults worry that this type of play teaches boys to be aggressive, reinforcing stereotypes about masculinity. But just like princess play, these scenarios are just ways to explore power.

Of course, not all children engage in either princess play or gun play, while some children engage in both.

Most pretend play has a gender component. For example, family play involves children taking on roles that can be gendered, which depend on the children's experiences, the stories they are exposed to, and the reaction of the adults, as, for example, some adults may stop children from playing family with multiple moms. Some groups of children will play two moms because that is part of their lived experience, either in their own family or in their community. Sometimes there are two moms because the players wanted two parents in the game and only girls were playing; the children's understanding of gender causes them to choose a family structure they are not familiar with rather than taking on a role with a different gender than their own. This is an example of their own-gender schema influencing their play.

Own-Gender Schema and Gender Expression

Own-gender schema develops in conjunction with superordinate gender schema. The term *gender identity* is often used to describe one's own-gender schema, how a person understands their gender within themselves. What I like about using schema as a model is that it more accurately describes how I see gender identity developing in young children. In the past, the field of child development used to view gender identity more as simply a milestone in development, following the work of Lawrence Kohlberg. In this view, at the age of three, a child realizes they are either a girl or a boy (Pastel et al. 2019). We have since learned it is much more complex and doesn't happen in a simple, linear way. Evidence shows that gender identity formation begins as early as twelve months when children begin to categorize people by differences and continues through the preschool years for most children (Pastel et al. 2019).

Meanwhile, gender expression begins in early childhood and continues throughout our lifetime. While gender identity is the internal feelings of an individual, gender expression is the external communication of those feelings. Identity and expression influence each other in a reciprocal way. A person will generally dress and act in ways that match their understanding of their own gender. Preschoolers often conflate identity and expression, and at times they can worry that a change in expression will affect their gender identity. This story will probably be familiar with many readers:

> Vanessa needed a new pair of underwear. I checked her cubby but there was no underwear from home. When I brought out the bin of extra clothes, there were only two pairs of underwear: a Teenage Mutant Ninja Turtles pair and a Spider-Man pair. Vanessa burst into tears, "No! Those are boy underwear!" She was inconsolable.

There was a time that I would have explained that clothing doesn't change who you are. I would have had Vanessa put on a pair despite her tears and reassured her it was fine. I now have a different response. I feel it is respectful to acknowledge a child's feelings about the underwear, not because I think it will change their identity but because I want to respect their feelings about their gender expression. In the case study, Q talked about avoiding feminine clothing when they first identified as nonbinary. Their gender expression helped them feel more secure in their gender identity. Once they felt more confident in their identity, they could show more variation in their expression. This is a cycle that other trans youth have described. Gender expression reinforces a person's gender identity regardless of whether they are cis or trans.

Gender expression not only evolves over time but also changes based on context. For example, using the example of clothing in the United States, a woman might choose to wear a dress along with jewelry and makeup for a formal event like a wedding but opt for more casual attire, such as pants and a shirt, to go grocery shopping. Similarly, adult men in the United States typically wear shirts and pants with minimal or no makeup or jewelry. These are all examples of gender expression. Despite significant changes in recent decades, societal norms for gender expression for women are broader than for men. Women can wear dresses, skirts, and pants; makeup or no makeup; and a wide variety of footwear without breaking social norms. Men, on the other hand, would be outside gender norms in most of our society if they did the same.

This discrepancy shows up in the costumes we often provide in group settings for young children. Young children notice the norms of gender expression in the world around them, creating their superordinate gender schema. Gender norms will vary based on a particular child's family and who the family interacts with. At the same time, I have found that children pick up on both the norms of their own family as well as the norms of society in general. A child may have a mom with short hair and still insist that girls have long hair and boys have short hair. This has played out in my classroom in several ways. Children show a preference for costumes that seem a little larger than life. They don't choose clothes that most adults would wear every day. They prefer fancy clothes or police, firefighter, or doctor uniforms. I have always found that feminine costumes are used most in my classroom. I often purchased quinceañera dresses that were fairly inexpensive in the stores in our neighborhood. I found them to be fancier and sturdier than the princess dresses from catalogs. Not all girls wore these dresses, and some boys wore them as well, but usually there was a small group of girls who wore them consistently. Tutus and skirts with patterns were also popular. Dresses, sparkles, and/or pastel colors would be used every day. Over the years I have also had blazers, clip-on ties, and menswear dress shirts. None of these were used very often. It's clear that feminine clothing was more intriguing than masculine clothing.

At the same time, I have found that boys frequently played with flowing scarves and shiny jewelry if they weren't read as *girl things.* The scarves with Velcro in the corners that I referred to in chapter two are an example. Children wore them as dresses, capes, and skirts. They would also use them to wrap or cover things. The patterns and textures were enticing for many children regardless of gender. But a dress made of the same material was used by a narrower group of children, almost always girls.

Many young children seem to worry about contradicting gender expectations. In my experience, many boys resist wearing a dress because they think *only* girls wear them, and they are not girls. The same is true for the roles they choose. Children will play a wide variety of roles, some of which seem to match their identity, but not always. They may choose a role without a distinct gender like a fox or bear. On the other hand, most children resist playing a role that contradicts their own gender identity. I rarely see a boy play mom or a girl play brother. Of course, even this is not universal. One boy I taught many years ago often took on the role of Grandma. Another year, I had a girl who would sometimes arrive at school in what she called her "man pants" and would take on the role of "Dad." But these exceptions are rare enough to be notable.

Like other cultural schema, a child's gender-schema development starts with a simplified idea of gender and gradually becomes more complex. Children generally take notice of those who seem to be part of their in-group. Many who are adults at the time of this writing developed a superordinate gender schema that sees gender as a dichotomy, following the societal norms of the time of their youth. Of course, there were individuals whose own gender schema did not match this dichotomy, but they were largely ignored by mainstream society. While research has shown that gender is far more complex than previously thought (Pastel et al. 2019), I find that cultural norms evolve more slowly. This can lead to parents or other adults feeling concerned when a child expresses their gender in a way that does not conform to the dichotomy of girls and boys.

I have found that this apprehension from some adults is more common when a child who is assigned male at birth dresses up in a way that is read as feminine, such as a boy wearing a dress or a skirt. There seems to be a fear that the boy in question will lose some of his masculinity, turn gay, turn trans, or at least be perceived as gay or trans. This mostly seems to be an emotional response. When I have talked to adults about these fears, most understand that putting on an article of clothing does not actually change a person. It's less of a worry that it will *change* the child, and more of a fear that it indicates the boy *is* feminine, gay, and/or trans. This fear implies that there is something wrong with being any of these things. And in reality, a child may wear an article of clothing for any number of reasons. It may be due to their identity or not; at the heart it is a child showing agency by making choices about their play.

You should be clear about your own values surrounding children's identity when caring for other people's children because your teaching practices stem from your values. I value diversity and acceptance, so I find it essential to help children see that gender expression has endless possibilities. In terms of pretend play, children may take on roles, act out scenarios, and wear costumes that may or may not fit various cultural scripts: a pink box or blue box, if you will. I don't think it is my role to tell children whether their choices are "correct" according to my idea of gender norms. As Jane Katch advises, "What I can do is keep reminding myself to ask questions and to listen, as openly as possible, to what children say" (Katch and Katch 2010, 390).

My values surrounding diversity and acceptance dictated how I introduced parents to my classroom. When parents were new to my classroom I talked about the array of costumes and props available to all the children in the program. I told them that I let children decide how they want to play because I was fostering their sense of agency. I made sure to mention that this might mean children engage in play that might include guns, princesses, superheroes, and so on. I acknowledged that there might be some uneasiness around some types of play and asked them what their thoughts were. I have found that most families are reassured when the educator is proactive in discussing what might come up. In my experience, the problem mostly stems from the surprise when their child talks about gun play or their son talks about wearing a dress, more than from the child's actions.

If a parent brings up a concern with you about their son wearing a dress or other feminine clothing when playing, you can ask them what their specific concern is. Once you know the parent's perspective, you can both acknowledge the parent's feelings and talk about the importance of the child's agency. You can articulate your values about diversity and acceptance. Then you can try to find a way to work together to support the child. If needed, you can refer to the National Association for the Education of Young Children (NAEYC) Code of Ethics, particularly ethical principles P-1.1, "We shall not harm children," and P-1.3, "We shall not participate in practices that discriminate against children" (NAEYC 2011, 3).

There is nothing wrong with a child expressing gender in an atypical way. All children should be supported in their identity development. In the story about Vanessa finding new underwear, I respected Vanessa's apprehension about wearing boys' underwear because it negated her gender identity. I would do this whether Vanessa was assigned female at birth or assigned male at birth. Respecting a child's identity includes giving the child agency to self-identify.

Another way you can support children who express atypically is by addressing peers' attempts at gender policing. Gender policing happens when a child actively tries to keep a peer from behaving outside the social norms of gender. Young children are just beginning to develop their superordinate gender schema, so you should avoid shaming a child who is policing others but instead teach them about the diversity of gender expression (Pastel et al. 2019).

If a child makes a hurtful statement, you can tell them that what they said might hurt other people's feelings and then check in with children who may have been affected by the statement. You can also have the child who made the statement check in the same way you might if the child physically hurt a peer. Children generally make these statements inadvertently as they develop their superordinate gender schema. As they become more aware of the impact their statements make, they can develop their impulse control to avoid hurting others.

Children are not born with their cultural identity, even though many of those identities arise from their biology. Children create their understanding of their identity—in other words, their cultural schema—by using different social scripts. This increases their own sense of belonging, leading to a sense of agency and self-efficacy. Meanwhile, children experience a variety of social scripts in group care. While other experiences in group care also contribute to a child's agency and self-efficacy, pretend play offers distinct benefits. Children share their internal mental imagery with others, which can add to their own sense of group identity if the play comes from a shared cultural script. When a child follows a script outside their own experience, they take on a different perspective, countering potential implicit bias.

You can empower children by helping them appreciate their own identity. At the same time, you can foster children's acceptance of other identities. You can listen to their ideas, whether in conversation or by watching their play. You can build relationships with the families in your program to learn more about the cultural identities that affect the developing cultural schemas of the children in your care. You can provide props and costumes for pretend play that offer windows and mirrors to your group. You can read books and tell stories that provide not only windows and mirrors but also sliding glass doors into lives the children might not otherwise experience. Finally, you can challenge children's developing implicit bias when it arises.

Children can build a positive sense of identity through pretend play, but this requires positive peer interactions. The collaborative nature of pretend play creates the potential for conflict. It's easy as an adult in group care to view these conflicts as obstacles to children's play. Over the years, I have found that I feel more connected and in tune with the children when I view these conflicts as opportunities to build the foundational skills needed to share power *with* one another.

CHAPTER FOUR

Peers Sharing Power

"OK, now it's my turn," Willem laughs. Elaine gets up from the ground smiling. They raise their pool noodles and Willem, as Darth Vader, says, "Luke, I am your father." Luke (Elaine) and Darth (Willem) battle with their sabers until Luke swats Darth's arm and he sprawls to the ground, letting his "saber" fly from his hand. Willem and Elaine laugh again and repeat the scene several more times, switching roles each time.

Later that day, Willem and Elaine are playing family. They argue over who gets to be the parent. Willem tells Elaine, "You have to be the baby or else you can't come to my birthday." Elaine looks dejected but says, "OK."

Children explore power in the realm of imagination. But children experience power in the real world as well. When thinking about adult concerns with power play, I like to focus on the real-life power dynamics in the play more than the scenarios chosen by the players.

Elaine and Willem take turns when sword fighting in the scenario above, but later Elaine takes on a role she doesn't want. Playing family may seem more prosocial than sword fighting, but it really depends on the real-life interaction.

In chapter one, I used the lens of power *over*, *for*, or *with* to look at the roles and scenarios children engage in. I want to use the same lens here, but this time I will look at the interactions between the children themselves. As the adults in this situation, our goal should be for children to engage in these interactions in a prosocial way. When Elaine and Willem take turns playing Luke and Darth Vader, they are sharing power *with* each other even as the play itself depicts the two trying to have power *over* the other. But when Willem tells Elaine she has to be the baby, he is exercising power *over* her.

If Willem knew Elaine was less adept at choosing a role, Willem could have said, "How about you be the baby and I'm your dad?" This puts Willem in the role that will lead most of the play while still involving Elaine. Exercising power *for* Elaine in this way, Willem would be scaffolding play skills. If this were the case, Willem would have suggested a different role when Elaine said she didn't want to be the baby.

Peer interactions like those of Elaine and Willem illustrate all four elements of power. Elaine and Willem are striving for a sense of agency, the ability to make choices that affect their world. If they are successful in having their ideas considered by their peers, it contributes to their self-efficacy. Children need self-regulation skills to be intentional in their interaction, not just acting out on their first impulse. Adults play a key role in assuring that all children can stay regulated while feeling seen and heard in peer interactions. When children feel seen and heard, they are more likely to make positive connections. In this chapter I will look at these elements of power together rather than address them individually. Instead I will focus on children exercising power *with* and *for* peers.

Exercising power *with* or power *for* a peer is essentially practicing consent. Consent may not be considered an academic skill, but I can't think of a more important skill to learn for success in school and in life. This skill is used in the context of pretend play but it also happens in any interaction with others.

I've used the term *skill* a few times now to describe consent, but author Lydia Bowers has helped me understand there are six distinct aspects of consent. She outlines them in her picture book series, *We Say What's Okay* (Bowers 2022). The series is focused on bodily autonomy or interpersonal consent. I have added a seventh aspect of consent concerning sharing space, so it also applies to group dynamics. The aspects are:

- We listen to our bodies.
- We check in with each other.
- We get permission.
- We accept no.
- We can say no.
- We are in charge of our bodies.
- We share space.

I find breaking down these aspects is extremely useful when considering what I can do to foster the self-regulation skills children need for each item. Self-regulation includes emotional regulation and accessing executive function skills, allowing a child to use their power in an intentional way. Children's developing sensory profiles also play a part in self-regulation. Young children are learning to use consent in their interactions. Each child will struggle with different aspects of consent, and most of these struggles will be tied to the underlying self-regulation skills and their sensory needs and preferences. I will address these skills and ways to facilitate their development, using one vignette broken up into short segments to allow me to consider each aspect of consent separately.

We Listen to Our Bodies

Lizz is playing with three My Little Pony toys. She is trying to build a block house that fits all three ponies. She wants to make a balcony but each time she has a block extend out from the house, it falls, knocking over the rest of the blocks. Lizz keeps trying but she is showing signs of stress, grunting and tensing her shoulders and arms. After her fifth try, Lizz cries and shakes her body, knocking over Aurelio's building nearby. Her care provider, Sonia, kneels down beside her. In a calm voice Sonia says, "You look frustrated." She extends her arms and Lizz leans in for a hug.

Listening to our bodies is the foundation of giving consent. We cannot agree to an interaction if we don't understand how we feel about it. Listening to our bodies involves interoception, emotional literacy, and using our executive function skills to respond appropriately. *Interoception* is the internal sense that detects that "something is off" so the need can be addressed in the near future (Chaves and Taylor 2021). It lets a person know when they are hungry, tired, calm, angry, and so forth. In a group setting, each child's interoception has a big effect on the group flow. A child who realizes they are hungry and asks for a snack is very different from a child who is hungry but doesn't realize it. A hungry child will have a smaller window of tolerance to deal with stress. Their ability to access their impulse control is lessened, along with all of their executive function skills (Center on the Developing Child at Harvard University 2021). Interactions with peers can be difficult. In the story above, Lizz didn't seem totally aware of her growing frustration, which led to her knocking over Aurelio's building.

One way I see interoception develop is during potty training. A child just learning to use the potty instead of a diaper may not notice the early signs of needing to use the bathroom. Countless times, I have been out on the playground with a child at this stage who suddenly calls to me, "I have to pee!" No matter how quickly we rush inside and get to the toilet, the child wets their clothes before they get there. The child did not consciously notice these interoceptive signals until they became overwhelming. Over time they will notice subtler signals, giving them time to get to the bathroom.

Interoception can also involve a child's need to move their body. Movement is associated with attention and joy. Young children require movement throughout the day for optimal development. If the adult is trying to have several children sit for more than a few minutes, some children will always feel the need to move. That skill of impulse control is early in development for young children. Expecting a typically developing three-year-old to wait a few minutes to move their body is appropriate. Expecting the same child to wait fifteen minutes is not and will likely result in a child who feels unsuccessful and an adult who is stressed from having to admonish the child.

Interoceptive development is dependent on executive function skills. In the case of potty training, when the child notices their bladder is full, they need the flexibility to allow them to pause what they are doing even

We have eight senses that allow us to interact with the world. Five senses are widely talked about: hearing, sight, smell, taste, and touch. The other three are less commonly thought of, but I have found that understanding these makes it easier for adults to attune to the children in their care. They are:

Proprioception: The awareness of body position and movements in space (Han et al. 2016). It gives us an awareness of where our body begins and ends and helps us control and coordinate different parts of our body. As proprioception develops, a child might:

- Break pencils or other writing utensils by pushing too hard
- Send sand flying in the air when digging with a shovel
- Sit on another child thinking there was space for their body

Vestibular: The sense of movement. It allows our bodies to move in space and to stay upright and balanced. As the vestibular sense develops, a child might:

- Fall out of a chair while sitting
- Bump into tables, doorways, and other children

- Need to shift their position frequently when sitting

The proprioceptive and vestibular systems work together. For example, when an adult sits in a chair, they typically take their eyes off the chair and turn a few steps before reaching the chair, relying on their vestibular sense to know they are placing their body in front of the chair. Then they squat down using their proprioceptive sense to gauge how far to squat before reaching the seat. This is noticeable when a chair has been lowered.

Interoception: The sense of internal sensations. It allows our bodies to recognize that we need to eat, urinate, seek comfort, and so on by recognizing the physical sensations of hunger, a full bladder, elevated heart rate, and more. As the interoceptive sense develops, a child might:

- Wet their clothes because they didn't notice they had to pee
- Eat until their stomach hurts because they didn't notice when they were full
- Hit other children because they didn't notice they were feeling uncomfortable with others around them until they were overwhelmed

if they are enjoying it and the working memory to rejoin the play after (so they feel less anxious about leaving the play). They also need inhibitory control to control the impulse to release their bladder immediately and to shift focus from playing to getting to the bathroom. In this case, I can support the child by asking periodically if they have to use the bathroom. I also tell them that I can hold the toy they are using or take a picture of what they are playing so they can resume play if they do have to go. I have found that this helps them pay more attention to their interoception rather than telling me they don't have to go just so they can keep playing.

I found supporting children in this same way to be more difficult when they need to move their bodies. As I mentioned, movement is necessary for attention. When a person is losing attention, their interoceptive sense will signal to their brain that movement is needed. The brain then signals movement. As adults, this may mean swinging our foot or shifting our position when seated. For children, it may mean rocking their body, leaning on a peer, tipping back in a chair, running, or many other actions. They are simply reacting to their sensory input. Obviously, some children need more movement than others to keep their attention at an ideal level. Each child's executive function skills vary, so their reactions to this impulse to move will also vary. Some are able to control the impulse to move so they can either wait or move in a way that is more acceptable to adults, which also requires mental flexibility.

As I learned more about executive function through my time as an educator, I was able to allow children to move more in group situations. One child might rock, one might lay down, and one might pace nearby. As long as they were not disruptive, they could move. I found that the group stayed more focused, and I was less stressed. This, in turn, allowed children to develop their interoception, which allowed them to self-regulate. In the past, I would find myself admonishing the same children over and over because the more I intervened, the less they developed their own executive function skills. Meanwhile, the less I tried to control the child, the less disruptive their actions were.

To support their interoception, young children need to have words to describe their internal feelings related to emotions. This allows them to connect the feelings in their body to the name of the emotion they are experiencing. At first, the vocabulary will be simple: *happy*, *sad*, *mad*. But as children master these words and the feelings associated with them, they can learn more words to describe the nuance of emotions. For example, there is a big difference between irritated and furious. Going back to the story, if Lizz started to notice her body's signals—the tensing of her shoulders, her grunting—she could have said, "I'm mad (or frustrated)." Recognizing this emotional state could have signaled to her that she should use the calming techniques she has learned, such as taking a few deep breaths, which could make her shoulders less tense. It could also alert Sonia earlier so she could provide comfort. This could be as simple as restating the emotion, "You're mad. The building keeps falling down."

What adults can do

Adults can foster interoception by encouraging a child to shift focus to determine how their body feels at different times. When they take a break from playing physically, ask them to feel their heart and notice how fast it is. Have them take deeper breaths and see if their heart rate slows. When they are potty training, rather than simply having a child try to go potty every thirty minutes, ask them every thirty minutes if they feel like they have to go potty. Remember to offer to keep the toy safe or take a photo so they can focus on how their body feels.

Meanwhile, the adult can increase a child's emotional vocabulary by reading books and singing songs about emotions. Some of the books may simply name emotions with a short description, but be sure to also read books in which a character experiences strong emotions. This allows you to talk about what the emotion feels like in your body. You can also talk about strategies to keep the emotion from being overwhelming (see strategies for fostering self-regulation on pages 22–23). And finally, acknowledge your emotions and those of the children in your care. "You're sad that Mom had to go to work." "I got worried when I saw you standing on the edge of the table." Try not to manipulate children with your emotions. I have heard adults use phrases like "It makes me sad when you hit your friends." When adults use phrases like these, it typically means that either the adult is playing on the child's desire to please the adult and is not actually sad or that the adult is truly sad and may be experiencing burnout and need therapy or some other form of help to address these emotions.

In the case of Lizz, let's assume her care provider, Sonia, has been building emotional vocabulary and doing daily breathing exercises before rest time. While Lizz is learning to name her emotions, in this case she wasn't able to do so. The best-case scenario would be if Sonia noticed Lizz's early signs of stress when she was tensing up and grunting. She could have offered, "You look frustrated. The building keeps falling down." In the story, Sonia came over after Lizz had already cried and knocked over Aurelio's building. Sonia then acknowledged her emotions and Lizz hugged Sonia. This experience allows Lizz to label her emotion and to co-regulate with Sonia.

We Check In with Each Other

The more children listen to their bodies, the more they can navigate their feelings and needs when interacting with others. Let's continue the story of Lizz:

> Lizz has calmed down and finally built a house with a balcony. Four-year-old Ross is crawling to the block shelf to get a block. As he reaches, his shoulder bumps the back of Lizz's head. Lizz yells, "Ross hit me!" "I did not!" Ross shoots back.

The next aspect of consent is checking in with each other. This is not an isolated skill to teach but rather a culture to foster. All people in a community can practice checking in with others. When a child gets upset, others should be encouraged to ask, "Are you OK? Is there anything I can do?" or similar questions. The adult can model this by also asking these questions. Because some children can get defensive if they feel checking in is an admission of doing something wrong, it is helpful to have any child ask these questions regardless of whether the individual was directly responsible for the injury. This is not about assigning individual blame but rather building a culture in which everyone is responsible for helping.

Individual responsibility requires the person to have an understanding of their own impact on others. Young children are still learning the concept of cause and effect and the related concept of intent versus impact. *Cause and effect* is the notion that one action leads to a corresponding reaction. If you make an incline steeper, a toy car will roll down at a faster speed. *Intent versus impact* is the notion that you may have an impact on something regardless of your intention. When Ross reached for a block, he bumped Lizz. Ross's intent was to get a block. The impact was bumping Lizz. Ross would need to understand his movement caused a collision and that his actions had unintended impact.

Aside from understanding cause and effect, children are still developing their proprioceptive and vestibular senses, which give them awareness of where their bodies are in space. Proprioception is the sense that detects where your body begins and ends. The vestibular system senses where your body is in motion. In the above example, Ross was focused on his hand and did not notice where other parts of his body were, so he was not cognizant of his shoulder bumping Lizz. The proprioceptive and vestibular systems are developing in young children. You have probably seen children walk into doorways and tables or seen a child try to sit in a space that is clearly too small. These are all signs that they are still developing their proprioceptive and vestibular systems.

What adults can do

Creating a culture in which everyone checks in with someone who is hurt allows for the various developmental stages of understanding cause and effect and intent versus impact as well as the differences in proprioceptive development. Anyone can check in by simply asking, "Are you OK? Is there anything I can do?" when they see someone hurt or upset. Children may get upset or hurt for reasons that have nothing to do with what others did, but of course we still want to help them. The focus is on the well-being of each group member.

Fostering a community where children check in with each other regularly takes off some of the shame a child may feel if they caused the harm. The goal is to have all children learn new ways to interact with others. If a child has pushed another child, the goal is to help both children feel heard. The one who pushed needs to learn that they can be heard without resorting to pushing. As children develop an understanding of cause and effect as well as intention versus impact, they can learn to take responsibility for harm they cause. Assigning blame and demanding a child say they are sorry may feel better for the adult but does nothing for children to feel heard or to learn skills necessary to get along in a group setting. A true apology requires the child to understand how they were responsible. Creating a culture where children check in with each other creates an awareness of the feelings of others, setting the stage to ask permission when they do want to interact.

We Get Permission

Going back to the story of Lizz:

Lizz is holding two My Little Pony toys, Rainbow Dash and Rarity, making them talk to each other. Heather walks by and watches Rainbow Dash ask Rarity to make her a dress. Heather reaches for another My Little Pony, Applejack. Lizz grabs Applejack from Heather, exclaiming, "I'm using it!"

A few minutes later, Bethany, who frequently plays with Lizz, walks over and kneels next to her. They make eye contact. Bethany picks up Applejack and says, "Hmmm?" Lizz nods her head slightly and Bethany raises Applejack, saying, "I'm done with my chores." Rainbow Dash says, "Let's play." Applejack hops around with Rainbow Dash and Rarity. Bethany and Lizz smile at each other.

Asking permission is often what we think of when we talk about consent. It is an important part, but only in the context of the other aspects of consent. Asking for permission may seem like simply saying, "Can I . . ." but expressive communication is more than just words. Along with spoken words, asking permission also involves gestures, facial expressions, and vocalizations. Vocalizations are the sounds we make that aren't words: "Hmmm," "Uh huh," "Oww," and so on. In the previous story, Bethany made eye contact, gestured to the toy, and then vocalized. This was asking permission because it is in the context of the friendship between her and Lizz. A similar exchange could happen even if Bethany wasn't able to speak.

In my experience, when consent is reduced to asking verbal permission, teachers simply instruct children to "use their words." This assumes all children know which words to use and ignores the children's social context. As an adult, I ask permission in different ways depending on the context. I hug my romantic partner without asking. I hug certain friends but not others depending on their own comfort level. In both situations, I also read their facial expressions and gestures to know whether the hug is welcome at this time. Young children can learn to do this as well. Insisting that a child use spoken words can lose sight of the actual goal of getting permission. The focus should be on getting permission regardless of whether anyone is speaking out loud.

In the example above, Heather did not communicate to Lizz that she wanted permission to play. She simply picked up the toy. It's not that Heather thinks she can do whatever she wants. It can be easy to slip into thinking that her taking the toy is a moral failing if we don't consider Heather's developing executive function skills. A child needs to develop impulse control to resist grabbing a toy they want. This also requires mental flexibility to think of alternative approaches and working memory to keep the goal in mind while using these approaches.

What adults can do

Adults should encourage the development of executive function and self-regulation skills as already described throughout this book. In addition, you as the adult can model asking for permission. Adults should ask children if they want a hug before giving them one or ask before touching a child or their creations. Even when an adult needs to touch a child to care for them, the adult can verbalize what is happening: "I need to change your diaper. Let me bring you to the changing table."

Make sure you are modeling different modes of communication. In our push-down of academics, there has often been an emphasis on spoken and written language. The truth is that all of us also rely on gestures, facial expressions, and vocalizations. Most preschoolers do speak, but some don't speak the same language as the others in a group care setting, others have speech delays, and still others will never acquire spoken language. Adults should encourage all modes of expression and help children understand their peers. This makes it easier for a child to interact with another child without adult help even if their modes of communication differ.

You can describe children's gestures to help children read them. "You're pointing at the basket of animals. Did you want me to pass them to you?" "She's moving away from you. It looks like she doesn't want a hug." You can do the same for facial expressions and vocalizations. Children pick up on facial expressions and vocalizations just as they pick up on words, but some children need assistance as they learn. Nonspeaking children sometimes use unique vocalizations. You may find that other children will pick up on the meaning of some vocalizations quicker than you.

Even with these proactive steps, children may need assistance in asking for permission. You can narrate a child's actions when they want something. In the story above, Sonia (the adult in Lizz's story) could say to Heather, "You want to use the pony. Lizz said she is still using it. Do you want help asking her?" Offering to help the child ask allows you to model how to do so. If the other child consents, you can leave them both to continue playing. If the other child does not consent, you can guide the first child through the next aspect of consent, accepting no.

We Accept No

Because she knows that accepting no can be difficult, Sonia takes an active role in the next part of the story:

Lizz grabs the toy pony from Heather and yells, "I'm using it!" Sonia comes over and says to Heather, "You want to use the pony. Lizz said she is still using it. Do you want help asking her?" Sonia then asks Lizz, "Heather would like to play with you. Can she use Applejack?" Lizz says (in a calmer tone this time), "I'm using it." Sonia tells Heather, "It sounds like she is still using it. Let me bring over the basket of ponies and see who else we have in there."

Sonia knew that Heather would likely have difficulty with Lizz's response. Accepting no seems simple enough, but it requires well-developed executive function skills. A child needs to resist acting on impulse. At the same time, they need to be flexible in their thinking, in figuring out how they might negotiate or in thinking of something else to play. And finally, the child needs the working memory to picture other options available. Without working memory, a child cannot be flexible because they can't picture alternatives, and thus they are more likely to grab the toy impulsively.

Accepting "no" also requires that the child be able to regulate their emotions. It can be disappointing to not get what you want. The less developed the child's executive function skills are, the more likely the child will become upset. If this happens, an adult should acknowledge the emotions the child is feeling. The child may become dysregulated—that is, reaching a state of fight, flight, or freeze. Until they calm down, the child is not able to problem solve. First the adult and child must co-regulate.

Co-regulation involves being in a shared space and relationship with a child as they regulate their emotions. While the adult cannot force a child to regulate, they can offer comfort, proximity, and coaching, creating conditions that enable the child to self-regulate. The adult may offer touch or comforting words, depending on the child's preferences. Some children prefer hugs or a hand on the shoulder, while others find comfort in holding a stuffed animal from home or having their emotions acknowledged. Proximity also varies from child to child. Some may want to sit in the adult's lap or rest next to the adult, while others like to know the adult is nearby but don't want them too close. It may be necessary to find a quiet place in the room to co-regulate. The adult can remind the child to take a deep breath or offer a wand for blowing bubbles. Once the child is calm, the adult can help them find a solution. If the child is not dysregulated, the adult can simply go into problem-solving mode, as Sonia does in the story.

What adults can do

A child is more likely to control their impulses and be able to accept a no response if they have the working memory to think of other items or materials that are available and then the mental flexibility to choose one. It helps to have the materials organized and stored in bins with labels so the child can see them easily from around the room. If a child struggles with working memory, you may also provide photos of some of their favorite materials. This can also help narrow the number of items to consider if the child has trouble making decisions.

The adult can support the child by bringing over alternative toys or offering to walk with the child to see what else there is to play with. I have also found that preschoolers are often just as interested in the social aspect of the play as they are in the toy itself. In other words, Heather may be just as interested in playing with Lizz as she is in playing with the pony. Sonia bringing the basket of ponies to Heather allows her to stay near Lizz and then choose a pony. Earlier in my career, I would have asked Heather to walk with me to look for the other ponies. Because I was failing to account for the social draw of being near Lizz, I could imagine Heather becoming dysregulated if I tried to move her away from Lizz.

Adults can support co-regulation proactively by teaching children some regulation techniques (see the strategies for fostering self-regulation on pages 22–23). Teaching emotional vocabulary is helpful too because children are more likely to calm down if their emotions are accurately labeled.

You can also create a sense of community by involving other children in the co-regulation process. If Heather was dysregulated and had her toy cat in her cubby, Sonia could ask Bethany to get it for her. Many children are aware of the comfort items of their peers. Eventually, children will get comfort items for one another without prompting. Having children involved helps them recognize their own power in the group and also may be reassuring when they are the ones who are dysregulated.

We Can Say No

Helping children accept when others say no is part of what they need to learn consent, but they also must feel empowered to say no when they need to. Lizz was able to say that Heather couldn't use the Applejack pony because she was using it. She was also able to allow Bethany to use it and join her in play. In this case, Lizz retained her agency over her play and the materials that were part of the play. Lizz did yell when she first told Heather not to use the pony. Sonia did not comment on the tone of Lizz's voice, but rather she restated her words for Heather ("Lizz said she is still using it"). This way Lizz knew her ideas were valued. When Sonia asked if Heather could use the toy, Lizz had the same answer, but she could now say it in a calmer tone. If Sonia had told her not to yell, it probably would have upset Lizz more because she would have felt misunderstood.

Earlier in my career, I found myself focusing on the way children said no. When Lizz yelled, "I'm using it!" I would have addressed Lizz to tell her to use an indoor voice, which would probably result in her getting more upset and raising her voice more to tell me that Heather is taking her stuff. Asking her to use an indoor voice would be me trying to control Lizz's tone by simply telling her to change it, which doesn't get to the heart of the issue. What I have found more effective is to show her that her message was heard, and then simply restate it with a more appropriate tone. When she feels understood, she can calm down, and I am modeling the same message in a quiet but firm voice.

I have found over time that many of the "challenging behaviors" that stressed me out were my own assumption that a child was choosing to act in a certain way rather than recognizing that a child can only use the strategies they know. Rather than simply telling the child what to do, I can help them learn more strategies—give them more tools for their toolbox.

It also helped me to keep in mind children's typical development of self-advocacy. Here is the sequence most children follow when learning to advocate for themselves:

1. Physically interacting with the other child (pushing, hitting, biting)

2. Saying no (with words, American Sign Language [ASL] sign, or gesture) while pushing

    a. The child's tone is usually harsh

3. Saying no (with words, ASL sign, or gesture) without touching the other

    a. The child's tone is still usually harsh

4. Using more complex language or gestures

    a. The child's tone can vary depending on how upset the child is

    b. The child may use emotion words to describe their feelings

5. Using I statements and more nuanced emotion words

    a. The focus is less on the other and instead on how it affects the child

    b. The child says phrases like "That irritates me when you poke my arm"

Of course, throughout a child's life they will use all of these strategies. They may find times in childhood or adulthood when they need to convey that they want something to stop in strong terms, perhaps using physical force or yelling. In situations that involve assault, for example, this may be necessary. There may also be times when chronic stress or trauma bring out these same reactions during events that may not warrant such intensity.

When a child is physically communicating their desire for someone to stop, they may push, hit, or throw things. An adult can acknowledge the emotions the child is expressing. "You're mad. You don't want them to take the toy." It helps to match the emotion a bit in tone and facial expression. This doesn't mean yelling at full volume, of course, but saying the child is mad with some conviction shows that you understand their feeling. You can then pivot to a calmer tone for the follow-up sentence, so it sounds more like this: "You're mad!" (said forcefully), and then "You don't want them to take the toy" (said in a calmer tone).

If a child is still pushing or hitting, you can tell them to stop: "You're mad! I can't let you hit them." You may have to repeat these phrases as you move in between the children to stop the pushing or hitting. Then you can add, "You don't want them to take the toy." The more heightened the emotion or the more dysregulated a person is, the fewer words they will be able to hear. You may even have to use a shorter phrase like "Hurting stops." This phrasing may sound a bit awkward if you are not used to it, but it is intentionally passive and nonconfrontational. You are not directing a specific child to stop hitting or pushing. You are describing an action that must stop rather than accusing the person of the action. In some ways, the child really is not in control of their action at this point so focusing on the action rather than the person can help deescalate the situation.

I have also started using baby sign (simplified ASL) for "mad," which is made by holding one hand like a claw in front of your face and moving it down. You can verbally acknowledge the emotion at the same time. This can be especially helpful for a child whose speech is delayed, but I find the strategy seems to help others as well.

As children become more verbal in their self-advocacy, their language gets increasingly complex and they start to use full sentences. Continue to encourage them to describe their feelings as well as stating what they want. You can model more nuanced vocabulary for their emotions. If they say they are mad, you can say, "You're feeling frustrated that they took your toy again."

While you are doing this, you can also model using I statements. The use of I statements can really help a child become effective at saying no. Earlier in my career, I would simply tell children to use their words. If Ben was poking Annalise and I told her to use her words, she might say, "You're bothering me!" Ben would get mad and the whole situation would escalate. In retrospect, Annalise was focused on Ben's actions rather than on her own experience.

This subtle shift allows a few things. Having Annalise say, "It irritates me when you poke me," gives her agency. She can consider her own actions, such as asking Ben to stop poking or moving away from him. Meanwhile, Ben will know what is specifically irritating her. If she had said, "*You* are bothering me," Ben might simply see it as an attack on him because it addresses him as a person rather than the action he did. Of course, the adult may help in this by guiding the children. "It sounds like Annalise doesn't want you to poke her. If you want her to talk to you, what else could you do?"

I find that the word *irritate* is a new word for most preschoolers so it can be helpful as they learn the skill of using I statements. It's also a pneumonic device, using an I statement with a word that starts with *I*. Using I statements allows each child to keep their sense of agency. If Lizz is irritated by Heather bumping into her, she can control her experience by moving herself farther away from Heather. Lizz does not have control over Heather, but she can have control over her own emotions around the situation.

Another factor in giving children agency is allowing children to claim temporary ownership over things. In other words, don't insist they share. While insisting on children sharing can make the adult feel like this will avoid conflict, it has negative consequences. It takes away the agency from the children. It is no longer their decision but the group expectation. I'm not sure the result could even be called sharing. True sharing requires the person with the toy to feel a sense of ownership and offer it anyway, and to do that the child needs to feel confident in their ability to have their own needs met. Involuntary sharing is simply complying with an adult. This can especially be true for children who have experienced trauma. They may often feel like they do not have control over what happens to them. A child experiencing food insecurity may never have been able to eat as much as they would like in any single meal. That child is unlikely to share food even if the family's circumstances change and they have plenty of food. Change does not happen immediately, but as the child learns that their own needs can be met, they will be more likely to share.

What adults can do

Learning to say no helps a child access the executive function skills they already have. The more a child can advocate for themselves and say no without hitting, the easier it is to control impulses. Most of the proactive strategies for helping children say no relate to emotional regulation.

Many of the strategies listed in the previous section "We Listen to Our Bodies" will be helpful here as well. Emotional vocabulary helps children to express themselves when they say no. As children learn to self-advocate without hitting, they use words to label their emotions. Increasing the variety of words allows children to express specific emotions, such as the word *irritate*.

Teaching sign language for the basic emotion words (*happy*, *sad*, and *mad*) is effective for times when a child is too upset to speak. Providing photos of emotions for children to point at can be helpful as well, especially if you have nonspeaking children.

Each of these aspects of consent lead to the final two related aspects. Children need to know that they are in control of their own body. At the same time, they must understand that when sharing space with others, they must also respect that each person is in charge of their own body.

We Are in Charge of Our Bodies

Lizz and Bethany have been playing with the ponies for several minutes. Lizz picks up Rainbow Dash as she takes on the role. "Watch how fast I can fly!" Rainbow Dash zooms back and forth, propelled by Lizz. Applejack flies after her, with Bethany saying, "Wait for me!" Bethany leans over so her toy can reach Lizz's. As she leans, Bethany's shoulder pushes on Lizz and they both tumble. They laugh, and now Lizz leans into Bethany, causing the two to tumble the other way.

I know that if this happened with the children in my care fifteen years ago, I probably would have told them they shouldn't push in the classroom. But Lizz and Bethany are both smiling. They aren't bumping into others. And it is a natural extension of the joy they are experiencing in their play. Earlier in this story, Ross bumped into Lizz, and she did not like it, and she told him. In both cases, Lizz is in charge of her body.

For me, this is the crux of the argument to allow gun play or other forms of power play. Play should be freely chosen, partly because play is recognized as a human right (United Nations 1989), but also because it fosters an understanding of consent. The way I see it, adults who prohibit gun play are focused on the power *over* dynamic within the realm of the child's imagination while simultaneously ignoring the power they hold *over* the child in the real world. This may come off as harsh, so let me explain how my thoughts have evolved on this issue.

I have reacted to gun play in three distinct ways over the years. First, I banned it from my classroom. I was exerting my power *over* the children, showing that my wishes were more important than theirs. However, the real-life lesson they might take away is that whoever has the most power gets to make decisions, regardless of the feelings of others. It also can send a message that if a child wants to play this way, their feelings are bad or unacceptable. In the end, this gives children an incentive to sneak around or lie to me. When I banned gun play, children whom I "caught" pointing a finger at a play partner would tell me, "It's a candy bammer." I had to either pretend I believed them or make them feel worse by interrogating them further. This is what Nancy Carlsson-Paige and Diane Levin call *guerilla war play* in their book *The War Play Dilemma* (Levin and Carlsson-Paige 2004). Banning this type of play didn't stop it. The desire to play out roles of power is pervasive. Adults exerting their own power to try to prevent it only makes it that much more appealing. If anything, once I permitted gun play in my classroom I think there was less of it.

When I first allowed children to play this way, the child care center still did not allow it, so I simply pretended not to notice when children played this way. If the director came into my classroom, I would tell children to stop playing that way and remind them that we don't play that way at school. But this was not a great solution. If a child pretended to shoot someone who did not want to play, I wasn't able to help them learn to ask permission, a vital skill for all interactions. Instead, I simply reminded them of the rule. Still worse, because I was essentially ignoring this play, I wouldn't always notice when a child was engaged in gun play with a child who did not want to play. I was missing opportunities to facilitate actual power sharing because I was worried about the power dynamic in the play theme. I was so focused on the pretend power dynamic that I was ignoring the real-life dynamic.

I eventually approached gun play in a third way, based on *The War Play Dilemma*. The third way is to allow gun play and then engage with the children. This allowed me to try to see the play from their perspectives. It also allowed me to help children negotiate when they did not get consent from other children. But most importantly, it helped me appreciate the play the children engaged in. I found that once I allowed gun play, I noticed the joy they showed. How did I not notice their smiles all those years?

What adults can do

Adults can facilitate children in controlling their own bodies by giving space and time for them to use their whole bodies in play, spending ample amounts of time outdoors as well as in indoor spaces that have room to move. However, many child care centers and family child care spaces are not designed for movement, despite young children's need to engage in movement throughout the day (Huber 2017).

Rough-and-tumble play is one of the ways children engage in movement. Rough-and-tumble play fosters physical, social, emotional, and cognitive development. Playing rough with another child can help reinforce concepts of consent. Because of the dynamic nature of the play, children must continuously assess consent. Simply saying they want to play rough at the beginning of the play is not enough. For example, two children may be enjoying roughhousing but then one child's facial expression changes when they get elbowed in the face. The other child senses a change in the sound and expression and pauses to check in.

The same is true when an adult is playing rough with a child. If a child is showing they are no longer enjoying the play, the adult should stop. The child may be hurt or overwhelmed. This includes when an adult is tickling a child. Tickling can be enjoyable but can quickly become overwhelming. Even adults often have a hard time knowing when to stop because the child will verbally say "Stop," but continue to laugh. These mixed signals aren't always enough to get an adult to stop—however, the laughter resulting from ticking is a physiological response and is not an indication of how the child is feeling.

Last, children hugging adults is a cultural norm that has been reexamined lately. Insisting a child hug an adult results in a child's loss of agency. Children should be able to choose whether they want to be hugged. Asking children if they want to hug, high five, or wave to greet someone is one way of showing that the child is in control. In my experience, some children may just want to look in the direction of the person. For some children, being forced to hug someone is a minor inconvenience. For others, it may bring up feelings from past abuse or cause the child to grow up thinking they are not allowed to refuse the physical touch of others with more power.

Of course, there are limits on being in charge of your own body because other individuals are also in charge of their bodies. We also have to share space.

We Share Space

Lizz and Bethany are playing with their ponies in the block houses they made for them. Tiffany and Alder come over to the block area to build "a whole forest." The two stand up blocks in the block area, soon covering most of the area. Lizz picks up the Rainbow Dash and Rarity toys, planning to have them race through the sky, but she sees that she is surrounded by this new forest. Unsure of what to do, she drops the toys and tells Bethany, "I'm done playing. I'm going to look at a book."

Some types of play take up more space than others. Many types of power play take up a fair amount of space. Reading books, coloring, or building with smaller toys such as Lego bricks or Magna-Tiles takes up much less space. There is nothing wrong with some things taking up more space, but there needs to be agreement from the group. Space is something we share, both the physical space and the soundscape.

Lizz's toy ponies are objects. Figuring out who is using them is fairly concrete. Lizz had three ponies by her building. When Heather grabbed Applejack, any onlooker could see that Lizz had two other ponies and a home for them. There can be gray areas around knowing whether a child is done with a toy when they set it down and walk away. Did they go to get something but intended to come back? But everyone can agree on what object is in question.

On the other hand, everyone shares the space in a room. Several children may have walked through the block area or even built in other parts of that space without interfering with the ponies' homes. In the span of an hour, a table might be a hideout for Transformers, a dinner table, and a place to color. Each space can be used for multiple activities, but they often can't happen at the same time in the same space. Needing to share space sets up a different type of conflict or negotiation. Sometimes a child doesn't like to be too close to children who are moving quickly or in big ways. Sometimes a few children who can build quickly take up most of the building space while another child is still trying to decide what to make. Some children get louder when they are excited, while another child gets stressed from the sound and looks for a quieter space.

In general, I have found that children strive to find spaces that aren't being used. If Heather went to set plates at the table and saw three Transformers underneath, she would bring the plates to a different table. At times, of course, conflict happens over a space. More often, a child will get the message that a space is not available to them.

What adults can do

Children who want to build a big building should be able to make a big building. At the same time, children who take more time to build should also be able to build. This is a situation in which adults may have to exercise power *for* some children. In the story, Lizz and Bethany wanted to move around to make their ponies fly. The forest that Tiffany and Alder built didn't leave enough room for them to do this. Sonia, the adult in the story, could ask Lizz if she was finding it difficult to play with her ponies with the forest right there. If Lizz said yes, Sonia could ask her for ideas: "What could we do so you could still play with the ponies?" It might mean moving the ponies or it might mean talking to Tiffany and Alder so they knew she needed room for her ponies to race. Discussing their space needs could even be a catalyst for the four children to combine their games.

If there is a recurring issue around space, the adult may want to try group problem solving later that day or the next day: "I've noticed there's usually a lot of people who build in the block area. I'm worried some people aren't finding enough space, and maybe they will decide not to build. What could we do so everyone can build if they want to?"

One more issue we must discuss in terms of sharing space is to consider children who get triggered by seeing certain types of play due to trauma, such as gun play. I am using the word *trigger* to refer to a stimulus that causes someone to recall a traumatic experience. If a child has trauma related to firearm violence, whether they witnessed an event directly or heard it or saw community members' reactions, seeing others pretend to use guns may be overwhelming. At the same time, some children who have experienced trauma are drawn to play out scenarios based on the traumatic experience, which can give them power over the event.

A colleague shared with me their specific experience related to this type of trauma. Many of the children in their program experienced collective trauma from the same event involving community violence. My colleague observed that some children wanted to act out versions of the situation while others were triggered by seeing this type of play. I should emphasize that all the families involved were also receiving other services, including mental health services. The adults had group conversations with the children, and all agreed that weapon play was not allowed when the entire group was together. The group's solution was that the adults would take a portion of the group outside to engage in weapon play while the rest stayed inside. This allowed children to choose their play while also allowing all children to respect the needs of others in the group.

Using a space is an embodiment of power. If one child or a small group of children uses most of the space, they are exercising more power than others. Sharing a space does not mean everyone uses the same amount of space all the time. Sometimes one activity takes up more space than another activity. Building with unit blocks takes more space than drawing a picture, for example. But an adult may want to step in if the same children are consistently using most of the space. In the same way that adults foster a culture of checking in when someone gets hurt, the adults can check in to make sure children are able to use the space how they want. Quieter children will sometimes defer to others playing more actively. I remember one year I had the same small group of children take over the block area. I would ask children their plan before they started playing, and I tried asking a few of the quieter children first. Two of them expressed interest in building with blocks. I rarely saw them play there and helped them talk to the other block builders about how to make room for everyone who wanted to build. Adults can also give a sense of shared space by including all children in the care of those spaces.

Children's sense of power grows out of their experience of power. Some of their earliest experiences will feature sharing power with peers. You as the adult also have a role in fostering a culture of consent in your program. Breaking down consent into the seven aspects outlined in this chapter allows you to foster the underlying self-regulation skills children need to truly share power with one another. Perhaps it seems counterintuitive, but when a child learns to share power with peers, it also empowers them. The same is true for an adult who shares power with children.

CHAPTER FIVE

Adults and Children

Three Ojibwe preschoolers, Jarvis, Migizi, and Luis, were holding long blocks as if they were rifles, tiptoeing through the room. I approached them, ready to remind them that we don't play with guns at our center. Before I could speak, one turned to me and said, "Shhh. You have to be really quiet. We're hunting." I knew hunting was an important part of their culture, but I didn't know much more than that. I backed off quietly, thinking this was the most respectful way to honor their culture.

Play is one of the main occupations of young children, and choosing what to play is probably their most frequent decision. As I stated earlier, leaving children space and time to play gives them opportunities to enter a flow state, which fosters self-regulation and executive function skills. Flow state is only achieved if children are allowed to determine what they play. If there are certain types of play that you find more difficult to allow, it may be helpful to appreciate children's play for its own intrinsic value, and to remember that the children playing may have a different perspective than you have as you watch from the outside.

The story above was from my first teaching job. As I mentioned in chapter one, my job was in a neighborhood where violence involving firearms was all too common. The center banned weapons play. The center also had a focus on culturally responsive care. This led to a dilemma for me that I first wrote about in my book *Inclusion Includes Us: Building Bridges and Removing Barriers in Early Childhood Classrooms* (Huber 2022). I was supposed to stop the children from pretending to use guns because the center saw it as a way of disrupting the cycle of violence in the neighborhood. I was also supposed to support children's cultural identity.

In the end, I chose to let the children keep playing. If I had told them to stop, I would have been telling them that part of their culture, hunting in this case, was not welcome at the center. In a sense, I was trusting that they knew more about their emerging cultural identity than I did. This may be an obvious example given that I am a white man and they were Ojibwe, but this plays out with every choice a child makes when they take on a role in pretend play. If I trust in a child's agency in developing their identity, I need to trust in their choices in play.

Children gain a sense of power through their pretend play. As I explored in the last chapter, they also need to experience power in real life. Chapter four focused on how children experience this with peers through the power dynamics that happen in play. Adults can also guide children's understanding of power by having children meaningfully participate with the group throughout the day. This can be done in two main ways: participating in decision-making and participating in caring for the community.

Participating in Decision-Making

In most group care, children have some involvement in making decisions for the group, but in my experience the involvement lacks true partnership with the adults. For example, if a few children ran away out of their classroom, the educators could have a group discussion with children to try to prevent it from happening again. But the power dynamics matter, and a group discussion can be an opportunity for an adult to exercise power *over* children or power *with* children as illustrated in these examples:

- A group discussion with adult exercising power *over* children might start like this:
- "Earlier today, a few of you ran from the room. That's not safe. I worry about you and want you to be safe, so I need you to be with an adult. If you wanted to leave the room, what could you do?"
- A group discussion with adult exercising power *with* children might start like this:
- "Earlier today, a few of you ran from the room. That's not safe. I worry about you and want you to be safe. I wonder what we need in the room so everyone can find something to play here. Does anyone have any ideas?"

When an adult is sharing power *with* children, their participation is meaningful. Here are five types of decisions common in group care that children can meaningfully participate in:

- Play
- Room arrangement and choosing materials
- Adult interaction
- Conflict resolution
- Group problem solving

Play

I started the chapter with a story about children choosing the theme of their pretend play, but children should have opportunities to choose what they play whether or not it involves pretending. Flow state is only achieved if children are allowed to choose what they play. It can also take ten or twenty minutes for children to settle into play, so children need at least forty-five minutes to really engage. At times, some children need an adult to help them either sustain play or find another activity, especially if they have not had the opportunity to freely choose their play in the past. Adults may have to support children in settling into play by asking them what their plan is, connecting them to children they could play with, or joining them in play.

Over time children will build up these skills and stay focused for longer periods of time. This happens not by children using these skills perfectly but by feeling the motivation to develop them over time. Unfortunately, the field of early childhood has drifted in the opposite direction. Adults preset activities that children are expected to do, taking away their need for decision-making. Often children are given less than thirty minutes to play, preventing most from ever reaching a flow state. It becomes a cyclical pattern. Children are not given opportunities to develop self-regulation skills needed for sustained play, and then adults keep children on these frantic schedules to "keep them interested." Lack of sustained playtime undermines children's self-regulation skills.

Taking this idea further, letting a child choose to draw with markers or with crayons while the child is assigned the art center is simply an adult exercising power *over* the child. Having uninterrupted time to play with multiple types of materials allows the child to choose who to play with, what to play with, where to play, and how to play. This is true agency. For children to exercise real power, they need the agency to act on their ideas. Materials should be stored in ways that children know where to find what they are looking for. One common way to do this in group settings is to create interest areas such as an art area, building area, pretend play area, and so on. The areas don't necessarily need to be where children engage in the activity. For example, if a child wants to draw a picture of their block building, they can get paper, markers, and a clipboard from the art area and bring it to the building area.

It does not matter how "playful" the adult-initiated activities are. They are not a substitute for sustained playtime. Adults can initiate activities that complement children's play, but they should not neglect a children's developmental need for play.

Here is a summary of ways to give children the time and space to make decisions in their play:

- Allow at least forty-five minutes of open-ended time to play.
- Ensure multiple materials are available.
- Ask children what their plan is if they lose focus.
- Connect children to others who are playing something that might interest them.
- Join children in play to scaffold play skills.

Room arrangement and choosing materials

You likely want to rearrange the room a few times throughout the year, and you can involve children in brainstorming about possibilities. Involving children in this doesn't just allow them to participate in the conversation; it ensures that they have the materials they need when they choose what to play. You could do this informally with children playing in an area, for example: "I notice you have to go all the way across the room to get water for the paints. Should we figure out a way to move the paints closer?" You could discuss things with a group at mealtimes: "I've been noticing the building area gets crowded. What could we do so there is more room for people to build?" You can also ask about it at a circle time when the whole group is involved. Circle time usually involves children taking turns talking with an adult facilitating, so it can allow quieter children to voice their ideas. Talking informally to one or two children might be sufficient if it's a small change that only affects children who play in an area frequently.

Adding or exchanging materials happens more frequently than rearranging the room. This gives you ongoing opportunities to involve children in decisions about their environment. They can also help decide where to put the new materials and how to label them. Children may remember materials that they used in the past but are now in storage. You could also brainstorm which types of loose parts they might collect at home that you could add to the classroom. Children may also have ideas for changing where materials go in the room. You can help prompt this by describing what you've seen, for example: "I notice you like to bring the pom-poms from the art shelf to the pretend play area so you can fill the jars. Should we change where we put them at cleanup time?" You may already move or change materials based on your observations of children. You would simply be making it explicit that children have a say in where things go. The more you do this, the more children will bring up ideas without prompts. The prompt is using power *for* the children until they gain the experience to share power *with* you. Of course, you must attend to health and safety concerns as well as licensing and other regulations. Young children also lack an understanding of budgets.

Here is a summary of the decisions children can make regarding room arrangement and materials:

- What materials can we add?
- What materials should we bring back?
- Where should materials go?
- How should we label them?
- How can we make an interest area bigger?
- Are there areas we should move?

Adult interaction

The way we as adults interact with children can invite or limit participation. Asking open-ended questions invites them to answer in a variety of ways. Acknowledging their statements by repeating them invites them to elaborate, for example:

"Tell me about your building."

"It's a castle."

"Oh, it's a castle."

"Yeah, a mean king lives there. But the good guys are gonna destroy the castle."

"It must be a mean king."

"The meanest king in the whole universe."

If you join a child in pretend play, ask the child what role you should take. Then follow their lead. You can suggest small changes to the scenario to help them if they seem stuck or to include other children, but respect the children's decision if they don't want to follow your idea. If you are not familiar with a role or scenario, you can ask about it:

"Who should I be?"

"Iktomi."

"I don't know Iktomi. What do I need to do to be Iktomi?"

"You have to trick us."

You can also give children openings to make decisions within adult-initiated activities. Children can help write or draw messages for the morning meeting. You can sing songs that allow for input ("What else does Old MacDonald have on the farm?") or ask children to choose songs from a songbook. You can do the same with yoga poses or other physical activities. Have children tell you a story while you transcribe. Then you can have children act out the stories.

Conflict resolution

When children run into conflicts with each other, you can lead them through conflict resolution. Betsy Evans (2016) outlines strategies for using conflict resolution with young children in her book, *You Can't Come to My Birthday! Conflict Resolution with Young Children*. You act as the mediator and give each child a turn to explain their side of the conflict. Then together you try to come up with a solution everyone agrees with.

First, children need to calm down from any strong emotions that have stemmed from the conflict. Children often become dysregulated during conflicts, as strong emotions activate the amygdala, the brain's survival center. We often refer to this as a "fight, flight, or freeze" response. When the amygdala takes over, it activates the limbic system, causing an individual to react with little input from the frontal lobe, the area in the brain associated with reasoning and problem solving. You will need to be more active as a mediator when children are developing these executive function skills. You also may need to bridge language or communication barriers such as different spoken languages or nonverbal communication.

The six-step process Evans outlines in her book allows children to identify their feelings, express their ideas, and listen to the perspective of peers:

1. Approach calmly, stopping any hurtful actions.

2. Acknowledge children's feelings.

3. Gather information.

4. Restate the problem.

5. Ask for ideas for solutions and choose one together.

6. Be prepared to give follow-up support. (Evans 2016, 24)

When two children disagree, the power dynamic of the pair is sharply in focus. In the absence of conflict resolution, one child will eventually acquiesce, whether due to the age, size, strength, or verbal agility of the other. An adult will need to mediate at first to mitigate the imbalance of power, but over time children will acquire the emotional regulation and problem-solving skills to come up with a fair solution without an adult. Social conflict starts as two individuals trying to exert power *over* the other but can become two sharing power together.

Group problem solving

Group problem solving, in which each child has a chance to voice their opinions or ideas, works well for airing recurring conflicts or problems. Perhaps the building area gets crowded so it is hard for children to build. Or maybe the outdoor play space is flooded so you need to come up with alternative ways to play.

If the group problem involves a conflict, you can do a puppet show that brings up a similar conflict without naming a specific child. Here is an example from when I became the teacher of a classroom at a small parent cooperative. I was getting to know the children, but they all knew one another.

We came in from outside. Jessica, Brett, and Seth took their raincoats off as quick as possible and raced to the bin of Playmobil toys. They each rifled through the bin until Jessica found two translucent items, a lantern and magic wand. She gripped them tight and shouted, "I got them!" Christian was still at the door, wrestling with the sleeve of his raincoat. He shouted, "No fair!"

This was my third day in the classroom. I watched this scene play out each day. One day, Brett found one of the pieces before Jessica, but regardless of who found them, the next ten minutes would involve a sequence of arguments over who had the translucent pieces. I used conflict resolution with the children each time, but the issue came up each day.

At morning meeting on my fourth day, I took four toy people and did a little skit where they all wanted a glass bead. I told the children that there was a problem at Grown-Up School and the four arguing over the bead were adults. I then took out another toy, this time a child. I told them that this was their teacher, and she needed their help. These grown-ups kept fighting over the glass bead. What could they do to solve the problem?

Several children suggested ideas, but Jessica and Christian spoke up the most. Jessica spoke the most about it not being fair that there was only one glass bead. She said that the grown-ups who didn't get the bead would be sad. Then Seth had an epiphany, "Wait! We had a million gold coins in our room a long time ago. Maybe we could give them some of those so there's enough for everyone."

Later that day, I found a bin of gold coins in storage. The next day at morning meeting, I told the children that I found the gold coins Seth was talking about, and I wondered if we should have them in our room so everyone could play with something shiny. They agreed and everyone grabbed some coins. There were still occasionally arguments over the two translucent items but no more than for other toys in the room.

I ended up using Grown-Up School frequently to solve group problems. Grown-Up School is an example of toy theater where toys are used like puppets. You can use hand puppets or simply draw pictures using stick figures. The key is to give children something visual they can refer to, so they don't have to rely on mental imagery. If I had just said, "I've noticed that when we come inside, some of you fight over the magic wand," children would have a harder time picturing the situation, limiting the depth of discussion and maybe even excluding some children who are still developing their ability to mentally picture past events. Also, using slightly fictionalized stories lessens the chance that a child will feel called out for their own actions. Children can feel attacked when their actions are brought up directly, in the same way adults can feel attacked, leading to defensiveness. This is why I statements can help when trying to think of solutions to social conflict (as discussed in chapter four).

I inadvertently used power reversal in the Grown-Up School discussions by having a child in charge. I originally did it because I had more adult figures than child figures. But I immediately saw positive effects. Children let their guard down, laughing a bit at these grown-ups. Whether using power reversal or not, and whether it's a puppet show, toy theater, or drawings, the real-life power dynamic is the same. Children are exercising power *with* one another to make decisions that affect themselves and their community.

Note, however, that group problem solving and subsequent decision-making can also lead to conflict. It is helpful to be prepared for this. Here are a few ideas:

- Can this decision have multiple outcomes? ("We will spend the morning outside, and we'll bring a blanket for reading books and playing Lego for those who want to do that.")

- Can the decision be made by consensus? ("It sounds like most of you want to go out, but there are a few who want to play with Lego, and Jeremy wants to look at books first. What could we do to include everybody?")

- If you choose to have decision made by a vote, how can you include the children who had the minority opinion? ("We only have time for one book before your families are here. *Snowy Day* had the most votes so I will read that, but you can choose a different book to look at or you can color.")

Participating in Caring for the Community

Making meaningful decisions gives children a sense of power, but taking responsibility for caring for the community is just as important. Caring for someone or something is one of the ways we exercise power. You can see this when children play parent, doctor, or firefighter.

As the preschoolers transition from lunch, four children are picking up the cots from the stack, reading the name (and symbol) and putting the cot in place for rest time. Two others are cleaning the lunch tables. Two more are sweeping the floor with me. A few children are coloring while a few others are throwing small pillows at one another and laughing.

This was a typical day for me in my classroom. I did not insist on children helping clean up, but I did provide them with the materials and take the time to show them how to help. There was always a bin of rags handy, a few small brooms, and towels for drying the floor if things got too wet. I could have washed the tables and swept much quicker myself, especially during the first few weeks when new children joined my classroom. They sprayed way more soapy water than necessary on the tables; they swept in every direction, scattering the crumbs. But I wasn't trying to be efficient—I was trying to create a culture where children took part in caring for the classroom. I was focused on giving them a sense of power.

When shifting my view of power, I have found that I needed to shift some of my terminology as well. Tiffany Pearsall, the founder of Play Frontier, an early childhood program in Washington, uses the term *ritual* rather than *routines*. She says, "Routines are always the same. They are like marching orders. Rituals are a relationship, a conversation. They might change depending on the day" (Tiffany Pearsall, pers. comm., March 24, 2024). This is closer to the anthropological definition: regularly repeated acts that embody the beliefs of a group of people and create a sense of continuity and belonging. What I like about using the term *rituals* is that it puts the focus on the desired goal. For example, we need the table set for lunch. How that goal is reached may look different each day. An adult could do it alone one day, a few children could do it with an adult another day, and all the children could get their own dishes another day. Overall, the power is being shared.

Here are some rituals through which children can care for their community:

- Self-care
- Care of the environment
- Cleaning
- Meals

Self-care

Self-care is fundamental in sharing power *with* children. When I first started teaching, I focused on self-care as a list of tasks children learn to do for themselves, because independence was the education goal. Doing the task was an indicator that the child had learned something. While that is one way to look at it, it doesn't value the empowerment children can feel when they engage in self-care. Focusing on accomplishing tasks can also lead to the idea that a disabled child is somehow lacking if they are unable to do a task on their own. Thinking of self-care as empowerment allows me to exercise power *for* children when they need my help and power *with* children when they can do things independently.

The following are some self-care rituals and ways to empower children:

EATING

- Talk with children about how the food they are eating keeps them healthy.
- Talk with children about what they eat at home, connecting their home life to their experience in group care.
- Involve children in meal preparation.

TOILETING/DIAPERING

- If a child uses diapers, ask them if they are wet so they focus on their senses.
- When a child has started potty training, ask them frequently if they have to go so they focus on their interoception.

- Once a child is mostly successful noticing when they have to go, have them decide when to go to the bathroom. (You can still have them try before nap or going outside.)

DRESSING

- Break down dressing into steps and have them do some of the steps: "You cross the laces and I'll finish tying your shoes."
- Use visuals for multiple-step processes like putting on winter gear.

Care of the environment

Caring for the environment involves many tasks that a child can help with. You may have chairs to be unstacked or bins to be set out to start the day. There may be signs to put up or deliveries to put away. Some art materials are stored away when not in use. Daily tasks will also depend on whether children all have the same start time or if start time is staggered. One year, four-year-old Bernie arrived right at opening and the next child arrived about an hour later. The first week, Bernie always seemed a bit sad having to wait for another child. He didn't seem very interested in playing with me until I found a way for us to connect through morning tasks. Bernie and I would unstack the chairs and roll out the carpet runners that went around the sensory table. Pretty soon, he would greet me by telling me which task he wanted to start with: "Let's do the rugs first."

Some materials are meant to be used up, especially art supplies and messy materials. I used to view throwing out and replenishing these supplies as one more task to complete before the children arrived. But that changed when I had the opening shift at a center when I was in my twenties. Getting to the center on time was enough of a challenge for me at that age, so I struggled with preparing the paints and making playdough. Meanwhile, only three or four children would arrive in the first hour. With the encouragement of my director, I wrote out a recipe for playdough using pictures. Every Monday, I set out the recipe and ingredients. At first, I would make it with the children, but I soon realized they could do it without me being at the table. I was available if they had questions or needed assistance, but mostly they did it on their own. Since then, I have always tried to find ways for children to help get the room ready for the day.

Cleaning

Cleaning up can involve children in several ways. Obviously, you as the adult never abdicate your responsibility for health and safety. You may need to rewash things sometimes, but allowing children to wash a table first is not a waste of time if you look at the task through a lens of power. The point of having children help clean isn't to have them do tasks for you. Nor is it a way of keeping children busy so they stay out of trouble, although both things may happen. The point is to give children a sense of ownership and agency over that space.

The following are some cleaning rituals in which I like to involve children:

- Sweep floors with hand brooms and dustpans.
- Wash tables with spray bottles of soapy water and rinse water, using rags, Swedish dish towels, or paper towels. Squeegees are tons of fun to use and work great for playdough, grains (rice, bulgur, etc.), or gooey materials; it can help to spray lots of soapy water on a surface and then squeegee it into a container.
- Assist in doing dishes, such as by loading and unloading the dishwasher.
- Wipe spills.
- Assist in doing laundry. If possible, have children help load the washer. If not, they can load the hamper, sort clothes, and fold laundry.
- Do some deep cleaning such as periodic washing of easels and chairs.

Meals

Sharing a meal together strengthens social bonds. When you serve healthy food, you are exercising power *for* children. But getting ready for a meal is also an opportunity for sharing power *with* children. Children can help set the table whether you use real dishes, trays, or paper plates. They can help clear the table, whether the dishes go in the garbage or a bus pan.

Serving family style is also a great opportunity for children to participate. *Family style* simply means that food is in serving containers that the children can serve from. Children with more coordination can help children with less coordination. If children bring their own lunches, you may be able to serve snack family style.

Sense of Ownership and Power

When children participate in decision-making and caring for their community, they develop a sense of ownership. They are not only included in a group but are also making a difference. They have agency. Contributing to their community in this way gives them immediate feedback. When they wipe up a spill, the table is clean. When a child remembers there are gold coins in storage, everyone has gold coins to play with. This immediate feedback increases self-efficacy. The more children feel ownership in the group, the more they are motivated to regulate their own emotions, and the more connected they feel to their peers. Of course, at times their self-regulation skills are not enough or their conflict needs adult mediation. These are times when you need to exercise power *for* children as they develop, but the goal is to share power *with* children. Here is how each of the elements is cultivated in this process.

Agency

Children gain a sense of agency as they make meaningful contributions to their group care community. But this does not mean that they can contribute without your support. There will be times that you are sharing power *with* children and times that you are exercising power *for* children. Both have the effect of increasing a child's sense of power. I have also found that these uses of power increase my own sense of agency as the adult. But exercising power *over* children decreased my own sense of power. The more I insisted upon compliance from children, the more they resisted, causing me to exert more control. This led to two predictable outcomes: the children were less motivated to "listen" to me (that is, to do what I told them to do), and they had less self-regulation skills. The more I shared power *with* them, the more they were motivated to engage in the community and the more they practiced self-regulation skills. I had more agency, and they did too.

For example, when thinking about how to involve children in cleaning in a group care setting, I want to start with the sense of community and then talk about specific tasks children might do. It is not just the adult sharing power with the children. The children are also sharing power with one another. This is what it means to be a community. Simply giving children a broom without the motivation to use it to care for the community will only go so far.

For children to be a part of a community, they need to feel connected to it. The group needs to include each child by recognizing each child's strengths, needs, and preferences (Huber 2022). And each child needs to feel a sense of belonging by knowing how they contribute to the group in a unique way. In my classroom, I used the guideline *We take care of each other.* One of the ways I used this was creating a culture in which children regularly did things for each other. If one child wanted tape but wasn't able to cut it, they got help from another child who could do it. At the beginning, the child would ask me and then I would ask the whole group if anyone was able to help. Gradually children would offer to help others with actions they could do, and everyone learned who to ask when they needed different types of help.

Taking care of each other also means that children understand that peers may play in a variety of ways, and they may also clean up in a variety of ways. Just as a wheelchair user may play "chase" differently than a child who runs, cleanup tasks may also vary. The wheelchair user may use a tall broom while the child who can kneel on the floor may use a hand broom. But the child who can run or kneel also has needs. Maybe they need help putting the marker caps on tight. All children have strengths.

Children also have preferences. There will be some things they like to do often, some things they do occasionally, and some things they have no interest in. I have known some children who would take on any task involving water, such as washing tables, paintbrushes, or toys. Other children mostly want to put things away in the pretend play area, staying in character a little bit longer—especially if they can be the Mom and the adult plays their child.

Materials should be stored so that children can access them independently. Store items in labeled bins on shelves accessible to the children. In mixed-age settings, some materials may need to be slightly out of reach or in a container that requires adult assistance to open. In these cases, the children should still be able to see the materials. There should be a variety of materials to meet the diverse interests and preferences of the children. All children should have some materials they can use easily and some that provide a challenge. For example, making marks with markers and paint is relatively easy but pencils require more dexterity. Loose parts offer a wide degree of difficulty depending on how a child chooses to use them.

The goal in setting up the environment in this way is that children can choose items they can use freely without having to ask for permission. Their sense of ownership is diminished if they must rely on an adult to act on their ideas. As educator Kisa Marx puts it, "We want our children to feel empowered to use the materials they do have without needing them rationed, as this behavior is as inequitable as not having them at all" (Facebook post, November 27, 2023). Agency relies on the ability to make choices, and selecting materials is fundamental to children's primary occupation of play.

Self-efficacy

When we give children agency to engage in meaningful tasks that they have a reasonable chance to succeed at, we are nurturing their self-efficacy. Children become more than passive participants when they are given real responsibility. If they spill milk, they can wipe it up. If another child cries, they can bring the child's lovey. They are an active part of the community. For this to happen, children should not be forced to do these things but be given plenty of opportunities to practice. This allows children to participate in ways they feel confident and thus are most likely to be successful.

The adult also must accept the child's attempts at helping. When cleaning, children often use far more soapy water than necessary. I simply let them know when I think we are ready to wipe and hand out rags while putting the bottle away. Then we all wipe the table together. I put some limitations on the cleaning, but I don't get stressed when they squeeze the bottle five more times after I say I think we have enough soapy water. Like elsewhere in life, sharing power *with* others means giving up some control over how things are done.

According to Albert Bandura, self-efficacy is fostered through direct experience, vicarious experience, encouragement from others, and emotional feedback (Bandura and Gervais 2017). It is helpful to use all of these strategies with a group of children because each strategy will be more effective for some children than for others (Gebauer et al. 2021).

DIRECT EXPERIENCE

- Child participates in care for the community or environment.
- Child makes decisions affecting themselves (e.g., what to play with).

- Child suggests ideas in a group decision-making process.
- Child voices agreement with a group decision.

VICARIOUS EXPERIENCE

- Child watches others care for the community or environment.
- Child joins group play and lets another child choose their role.
- Child watches a group make a decision together.

ENCOURAGEMENT FROM OTHERS

- Adult breaks down a task into smaller steps for a child to increase success (e.g., first give the spray bottle, then exchange it for a rag).
- Peers or adults acknowledge a child's effort:
    - "Thank you for cleaning the table."
    - "You worked hard on that building, and you finally got it to stay up!"
    - "You both wanted to be Hulk and you solved the problem by being Thor."

EMOTIONAL FEEDBACK

- Child feels proud after accomplishing a goal (e.g., making a tall building).
- Child feels a sense of trust with peers after they work together.

Using Bandura's insights, there are a few things you can do as an adult to foster self-efficacy. For children to experience success in the environment, they need tools that accommodate their smaller arms and less developed motor skills. Here are a few tools that have worked well for me:

- Hand brooms with individual dustpans
- Bucket with a small amount of soapy water and rags
- Bath towel–sized rags (for when the bucket tips or for other big spills)
- Squeegees for hard-to-clean messes

Do not force children to join in; rather, create conditions for them to want to join in. Some children prefer to watch others do a task for a while before attempting it themselves. Vicarious experience is one way children gain confidence; trust the process even if you don't see the results for a few weeks. You can also turn tasks into collaborative efforts. If Lars is watching two others wipe shaving cream off a table with squeegees, you can ask, "Lars, do you want to hold this bucket to catch the shaving cream?" Collaboration provides a child an entry point that might require less coordination or skill while also inviting encouragement from others as the children work together.

Cleaning and caring for the environment are concrete so it can be easier to see children's varying involvement in the process, but the same dynamics happen in community decision-making. Some children will be more vocal and come up with ideas faster than others. Some children may want to contribute ideas but need a little more time to think. Still others may just want to observe the conversation. To make sure everyone is part of the group decision, you can slow the process down by asking questions like "Lars, it looks like you're thinking of an idea. What do you think?" If other children chime in, you can say, "Hold on, let's give Lars a chance to think of his idea." If you notice Lars finds it hard to come up with ideas under pressure, you could also talk to him one-on-one a little before the group conversation.

Self-regulation

The more children have confidence that they can contribute to the community and that their contributions make a difference, the more they will exercise power *with* others. Children feel a sense of control, which can cool the temperature of the room so they are calmer and have fewer meltdowns.

Being involved in classroom decision-making assists with self-regulation because children feel a sense of ownership and are less likely to get upset about a decision where they felt heard, even if they don't get their way each time, knowing there will be a next time. This comes with practice, so you can help by giving children opportunities to weigh in on decisions whenever possible. Children can also be part of the decision-making process when there is a conflict between two children. Conflict resolution with an adult as the mediator is a great way for children to feel heard, learn to negotiate, and be involved in the solution.

Additionally, caring for the community and environment promotes self-regulation in several interrelated ways. It often involves heavy work, which is any action that involves a counter force pushing against a child's force (Huber 2017). Sweeping or wiping involves friction as children move their arms. Stacking chairs or moving cots involves counteracting gravity by lifting something heavy. In truth, one major reason that I started involving children in more of the care of our environment was to assist in their self-regulation. A steady diet of heavy work makes it easier for a child to regulate their arousal level.

Children's self-regulation is dependent on their sensory diet. A sensory diet is the sensory input a person receives in a given day, as well as their response to that input (Huber 2022). Everyone has sensory receptors that receive information throughout their day. That input can cause mild stress designed to get a response. For example, when my interoceptive receptors notice I am hungry, I feel slightly uncomfortable and find a snack. If I am unable to eat immediately, the stress is generally mild enough that I can still carry on. However, other stressors such as loud noise or unwanted news can push that stress to an intolerable level, and I get mad. In other words, I get hangry.

Most people have ways to modulate this stress with the actions (occupations) that they do during the day. Most people don't consciously think of these things as responses to sensory input, but rather notice the emotional regulation certain occupations have. Heavy work and repetitive actions both have a regulating effect. Going for a walk, knitting, tinkering, or other repetitive movements are ways many of us self-regulate. We can also engage in heavy work such as cleaning or exercising. A child who sits at the sink with water running over their hands has found sensory input that works for them. I had at least one child like this in my care every year. Before learning about sensory diets, I would tell them to stop playing in the water and to find toys to play with. Now, I see a child who needs a certain type of input. I make sure to offer materials in the room that might meet that need: warm water in a sensory table, shaving cream, finger paint, and similar items. I also know that they will wash their hands more often than the other children.

Children's sensory diet usually isn't set until age six (Huber 2022). Young children tend to get overwhelmed easily and often need an adult to help them regulate. This is partially the result of children not knowing what is enough input to keep them interested without being too much. They are also still learning which occupations and actions help them regulate when they are overwhelmed. Many forms of play offer the repetitive motions or heavy work needed to regulate. Most children just need time, space, and the understanding of the adults to figure out what they need. Unfortunately, play that involves heavy work is often discouraged indoors because children use their whole body. Adults often encourage children to sit down with toys or art materials. But children who need heavy work to regulate would be better served by making art with boxes and other three-dimensional materials that require the artist to move around their creation. Children also use their whole body when they take on pretend play themes such as superhero and firefighter. For individuals with autism, sensory processing disorder, or other neurodivergence, a sensory diet may also involve more intentional strategies to keep them regulated. Some children require an occupational therapist or other specialist to work out what their needs are. All children need a diet of sensory experiences as well as heavy work and repetitive motions to keep them regulated.

I often found cleanup time to be one of the most stressful periods in my work with children. Looking at it through a lens of sensory diet, it is easy to see why. It is loud and visually busy, and children are often in close contact or bumping into each other. Meanwhile, there is little recourse for someone who is overstimulated besides hiding. I often interpreted this sensory need as a child trying to shirk their responsibility. I was turning a developmental issue into a moral one. As I shifted my focus to building community, I found children to be more focused and regulated. Children started wiping up spills without being asked, even wiping up spills caused by others. I had more time to interact with children rather than being the one who did most of the cleaning.

Even the children who didn't help clean up stayed more focused. The children who were throwing pillows were only doing it with others who wanted to. There were rarely children who couldn't find something to do. And when there were, I could go help that child while the others cleaned. Each child and adult became active members of the community. No one person did everything, but each person contributed. Each child belonged to the community in their own unique way.

Connection

Creating a culture in which children share power with adults and peers leads to a feeling of trust and a sense of belonging. As Milton Mayeroff (1990, 2–3) put it in his book *On Caring*, "In the sense in which a man can ever be said to be at home in the world, he is at home not through domination, or explaining, or appreciating, but through caring and being cared for." Not everyone's way of caring for the community and environment will look the same. To foster belonging, the adult must strive for inclusion, creating a variety of opportunities for children to participate but without insisting on participation. I once had an autistic preschooler who was nonspeaking who mostly wandered around the room humming while some children swept up wood pellets from the sensory table and others washed the tables or put blocks away. She would glance over occasionally and, when no one was nearby, she would pick up one block, put it on the shelf, and then go back to humming. In this way we all worked as a community, but everyone did not do the same cleanup job.

When I shifted my expectations from individual responsibility to community responsibility, the tone shifted. Children found a role they wanted, and I helped orchestrate the endeavor. Preschool children often imitate each other. One time a child picked up the Lego basket and walked around to have others put the Lego bricks in. Soon several children had found baskets that were meant for various toys and were walking around, but then there were no children to put toys in the baskets. I sat on the floor and picked up a toy and called out, "I have a lion!" The child with the animal basket came over. Soon I was interacting with multiple children. And because I was doing it, this task suddenly carried a new importance. A few children joined me, calling out, "I have a Bristle Block" or "I have a car." Soon we were all smiling and engaging with one another. Of course, it doesn't always go this way, but the shift in my attitude kept me from thinking of individual children as falling short. Instead, I thought about what I could do to motivate children to care for the community.

I shifted my attitude by looking at cleanup time as more than a series of tasks but rather as opportunities for collaboration. Psychology professor Barbara Rogoff differentiates between chores and collaboration. Chores are assigned by adults for children to do, and collaboration is when children and adults work together. She finds that children who collaborate with adults are more likely to share power *with* others (Rogoff 2015). Children who are assigned chores are more likely to use power *over* other children.

You can find many opportunities to collaborate with children in the upkeep of the group environment. Rogoff offers some basic guidelines when doing this:

- Include everyone but expect each person to participate differently.

  ◦ Adults pitch in together with children.

- Value everyone's contributions.

  ◦ Treat helping as normal. (Don't heap on praise such as "Good job.")

- Support children's initiative.

  ◦ Facilitate children's effort. (If it's a new task, show them or have another child show them.)

Think about the learning environment not as a static backdrop you create for children but as a dynamic space that requires participation from children and adults. While you can set up the initial environment, it is continuously evolving. Materials get used up. Interests change. Things get spilled. You can apply Rogoff's guidelines to almost any task that comes up in group care.

Of course, all this collaboration leads to conflict when several children want to do the same task. I have found that many children really sense the power in helping and want to be part of it. When I first had children take on some of the cleaning that I was doing, I had just one broom. Children were always fighting over who would use it. The same was true when children wanted to help wipe up spills. I found that I needed at least four hand brooms (for a class of ten). I also needed at least three rags per child so there would be enough before the next laundry load. I had a stack of towels to wipe up bigger spills or the enthusiastic use of soapy water. Having all these in place allowed children to work at the same time, whether collaboratively or in parallel.

There are many ways for children to have real power in group care. The first step is to think through your values around power and control. In retrospect, I first viewed power as a pie with only so many slices. Giving others power meant less power for myself. I was giving up power. Operating from this perspective, any adult could feel a loss of control.

I now view power more like a candle. I don't lose the flame on my candle, but as other candles are lit, the room gets brighter. The power of the group surpasses any power I could exert on my own. Having children participate in decision-making and caring for the community empowers all involved. Sharing power with children increases their agency without diminishing mine. Rather than giving up control, I was able to focus on the things I did have control over.

I have heard educators and administrators working with young children say that children need to learn to follow directions, and demanding compliance is portrayed as preparing children for school. But this is not teaching self-regulation, a fundamental part of academic success. Self-regulation is not sitting for circle time for fifteen minutes. Self-regulation is accessing your executive function skills to achieve a self-imposed goal (Center on the Developing Child at Harvard University 2021), the very definition of agency (Bandura and Gervais 2017). If someone is facing a lean winter, you don't starve them to prepare—you teach them how to garden.

Before you can nurture a garden, you need to nurture yourself. When you feel powerless, you can't empower others. You will need to reflect on ways to find your own agency and identify outside resources to assist you.

CHAPTER SIX

Your Own Power

Maggie scribbles on a sticky note and hands it to her mom. This is mom's cue that Maggie is playing Boss. "Is this my to-do list?" The Boss (Maggie) responds, "Yes!" Mom decides to poke at the power roles. "Can I do it later? I wanted to play." But the Boss is having none of it. "No! You need to do it now!"

I started the book with a story about Maggie, the Boss, ordering her mom around and eventually firing her. I then explored the experience of power from the child's point of view. Children's sense of power, however, is intricately tied to the adults in their lives. And those adults also experience power. Exploring power is foundational for children's healthy development, but if this is to happen, the adults in the child's life need to feel confident enough to allow this exploration. Maggie's mom may not have played this way if she had just lost her job. It may have felt dispiriting for her. The more empowered the adults feel, the more likely they are to exercise power *with* and *for* children rather than power *over* them.

When I first reflected on how children play with power, especially in the context of gun play, my own sense of power affected my understanding. As I said in chapter five, the first center where I worked banned gun play, and yet anti-racism was part of the mission of the larger agency. I saw a dilemma between the cultural experience of the Indigenous children whose families hunted and the broad prohibition that did not allow children to pretend to use guns. But I did not believe that I could bring this up to my director because I was relatively new in the field. This lack of self-efficacy kept me silent.

Meanwhile, I saw the violence in the community where I worked and knew it was beyond my control. Banning gun play could make me feel in control of something, even if it was just my own classroom. Over time, I realized that my work providing care for families was my contribution to the community. I had control over how I interacted with the children and their families. I gained confidence and took note of which of my actions fostered connection to children.

At first, this confidence led me to turn a blind eye to children engaging in gun play. Over time, I saw children thrive in ways that I illustrate throughout this book. This experience and having more years in the field of early childhood care and education gave me more confidence. Reading *The War Play Dilemma* (Levin and Carlsson-Paige 2004) and then discussing it with others was a turning point for me. I suddenly had others who shared a similar viewpoint with me. And, honestly, being a white male gave me some level of credibility that I did not necessarily earn.

In the subsequent decades, I have read and talked to others—notably Minnesota educator Kristen Wheeler Highland—who broadened my perspective to consider power play as a whole and not just gun play. This caused me to allow all types of pretend play in the programs I have been a part of. In other words, my own sense of power affects my decision to allow children to experience power, both in their imagination and in their communities. It is only fitting that I conclude this book by illustrating how each of power's elements—agency, self-efficacy, self-regulation, and connection—apply to your power as it relates to your relationship with your practice.

Your Agency

My hope is that this book will give you a sense of power to reflect on your practices with children. Books like this one and the resources listed as references for this book can give you more information. Just as importantly, notice the children you work with. What gives them a sense of power? Where do they run into conflict? What executive function skills could you help foster so they can better share power with others? As you reflect on these questions, consider how the answers might inform changes in your own practice. If you want to make changes in your practice, you must start with imagining the change. What would it look like if you enacted this change? Might you have a closer connection with certain children if you approached their play with curiosity? What would it look like if you exercised power *with* children more and power *over* them less?

How you use your agency will depend on your supervisor's attitudes toward power play. If your supervisor does not allow certain types of power play, find ways to advocate for children to choose their own play. Offer to give a list of resources to your supervisor. If you are in a larger program, perhaps you could find a few teachers who are interested in reading some books with you, and then propose changes together.

Even if you are not able to allow gun play currently, are there ways you can foster the skills necessary for a culture of consent? Are there ways you could share real power with children, allowing them to care for the community and participate in making decisions?

Your Self-Efficacy

Just as we foster children's self-efficacy as they gain agency, we can do the same for ourselves. Yet I have found it easier to do this for children than to do it for myself. I imagine this is common for those of us in caring professions because we tend to focus on the needs of others. It might be helpful to remember the four ways to foster self-efficacy (Bandura and Gervais 2017): direct experience, vicarious experience, encouragement from others, and emotional feedback. It might look a little different when we focus on ourselves, rather than the children in our care.

Direct experience

Direct experience builds confidence when those experiences are mostly successful. Therefore, you should find success in the smaller steps of a task. Don't try to make big changes all at once; try taking smaller steps. Maybe start by allowing superhero play but not gun play. Or allow gun play on the playground but not in the classroom. As you get comfortable with a change, think about the next step.

Vicarious experience

It can be encouraging to see others achieve success in the thing you want to accomplish. Connecting with a network of other educators is a great way to learn about new things. If you work with others, your coworkers might make up this network. You could also meet others on social media or at conferences and local associations. If anyone in your networks has changed their own approach to power play, you can ask about their experiences.

You can also read books such as *Rethinking Weapon Play in Early Childhood: How to Encourage Imagination, Kindness, and Consent in Your Classroom* by Samuel Broaden and Kisa Marx (2024), *Pursuing Bad Guys: Joining Children's Quest for Clarity, Courage and Community* by Donna King (2021), *Under Deadman's Skin: Discovering the Meaning of Children's Violent Play* by Jane Katch (2001), or *Bad Guys Don't Have Birthdays: Fantasy Play at Four* by Vivian Gussin Paley (1988).

Hearing about the experiences of others can give you ideas to try. Or knowing that others have made this change could give you the confidence to picture yourself making similar changes.

Encouragement from others

One thing a social network can give you that a book or podcast can't is encouragement. Getting feedback from others can inspire you even if you are not always sure of yourself. Look for children's responses as well. Are certain children participating in the group more as you make changes? Are you making new connections? I know behaviors I found challenging suddenly became fascinating as I changed my attitude. I grew closer to children I had struggled with.

Emotional feedback

You will go through different emotions as you change your practice. Sometimes you will feel great about the way things are going. But in the moment, you might feel uncomfortable. I know it was hard for me when I first saw the children playing Darth Vader and Luke battling to the death.

It can help to keep your hands busy. For example, when a few Transformers start blasting each other, you're less likely to make a comment if you are drawing with another child. Even so, you may fall into old habits and tell a child to stop blasting, but then immediately regret it. Having this self-awareness is still a step toward change. Think how you could react next time, and slowly you will start to react that way.

Your Self-Regulation

Self-regulation is critical for changing your practice. Of course, your dys-regulation probably doesn't look the same as a young child's. When I am dysregulated with a group of children, I usually start demanding children comply, simply telling them to do things because I said so. In a sense, I try to assert my control because I am not feeling in control. I might raise my voice or not pause long enough for a child to respond to me.

Reflective practice can help with your own dysregulation. If I feel something didn't go the way I wanted, I can reflect later on which executive function skills I may or may not have accessed in myself:

IMPULSE CONTROL (INHIBITORY CONTROL)

- Did I take a deep breath before responding?
- Did I use a calm tone of voice (or wait until I was able to)?

FOCUS (INHIBITORY CONTROL)

- Did I focus on what the child's behavior communicated about their needs in the moment?
- Did I focus on a child's attempt rather than the impact? Were they simply trying to help when they spilled the milk?
- Could I spend more time observing the children instead of frequently correcting behavior?

THINKING THROUGH POSSIBLE IDEAS (MENTAL FLEXIBILITY)

- What other ways could I have responded?
- Was there something I could have done proactively?

DEALING WITH CHANGE (MENTAL FLEXIBILITY)

- Can I remind myself that this is new for me?

WORKING MEMORY

- How can I remind myself of the overall goal rather than small setbacks?

REGULATION

- Do I find time to breathe deeply throughout the day?
- What phrases can I use for self-talk to keep myself regulated?
- Are there quotes or pictures I could put on the wall that would help?
- Is there someone I can talk to later to vent any residual feelings?

When you are regulated, you are more prepared to engage in power reversal play with children. When Maggie the Boss fires her mom, it is a healthy way for her to try out her power, but it requires her mom to be in a place emotionally where she can also appreciate the play. An adult who feels powerless may be less receptive to having a two-year-old firing them. When you can engage in this type of play, celebrate that this is a sign the child trusts you.

Your Connection to Others

Your connection to others is key to your success in any changes you may make after reading this book. As I mentioned in the self-efficacy section of this chapter, you can connect to other educators through books, magazines, and social media, as well as in person through conferences, associations, or informal social groups.

It's also essential to connect with families if you want them to accept the changes you make. Let them know any benefits you discover in the process. My hope is that this book offers several ways to talk about power play. It is important to be aware that your cultural identity affects how you view children, as well as how you learn new information and adapt to change. Each parent or guardian has their own cultural lens that affects their reactions as well. Some families will want information from experts, some will want emotional reassurance, and some will want to observe or see documentation of what power play looks like.

Your connection to children will help guide you as you make changes in your attitude toward power play. My initial uneasiness about gun play and princess play were alleviated by watching the effect this pretend play had on children. My discussions with Q and A and several others during the writing of this book have also solidified my belief that children use power play to gain their own sense of power.

When Eve Trook described the three ways adults use power with children, she said that when the adult shares power with a child, "the child and teacher are liberated" (Trook 1983, 2). Borrowing from educator Kisa Marx, a scarcity mindset—whether toward materials or control of group care—leads adults to focus on keeping control. A liberated mindset leads to a focus on possibilities.

Truly our power resides in our imagination. ✶

References

American Medical Association. 2024. "Firearms as a Public Health Problem in the United States—Injuries and Death H-145.997." Accessed October 7, 2024. https://policysearch.ama-assn.org/policyfinder/detail /H-145.997%20?uri=%2FAMADoc%2FHOD.xml-0-554.xml.

Australian Children's Education and Care Quality Authority. 2018. "Supporting Agency: Involving Children in Decision-Making." www.acecqa.gov.au /sites/default/files/2018-04/QA1_SupportingAgencyInvolvingChildren inDecisionMaking.pdf.

Bandura, Albert, and Michael Gervais. 2017. "Dr. Albert Bandura on the Theory on Creating Human Results." *Finding Mastery* (podcast). August 30, 2017. https://findingmastery.com/podcasts/albert-bandura.

Bernt-Santy, Heather, and Stephanie Goloway. 2024. "Happily Ever Resilient with Author Stephanie Goloway." *That Early Childhood Nerd* (podcast), episode 314. March 20, 2024. www.thatearlychildhoodnerd.com/podcast /episode/1f0e6907/nerd_0314-happily-ever-resilient-with-author -stephanie-goloway.

Bishop, Rudine Sims. 1990. "Mirrors, Windows, and Sliding Glass Doors." *Perspectives: Choosing and Using Book for the Classroom* 6, no. 3 (Summer): 9–11.

Bowers, Lydia. 2022. *We Say What's Okay* series. Illustrated by Isabel Muñoz. Minneapolis, MN: Free Spirit Publishing.

Broaden, Samuel, and Kisa Marx. 2024. *Rethinking Weapon Play in Early Childhood: How to Encourage Imagination, Kindness, and Consent in Your Classroom*. New York: Routledge Press.

Burton, Cayley. 2021. "'This Is a Different Kingdom'": A Case Study of Gender-Creative Feminine Expression during Princess Play." *Heliyon* 7 (5): e06994.

Center on the Developing Child at Harvard University. 2021. *Three Principles to Improve Outcomes for Children and Families*, 2021 Update. www.developingchild.harvard.edu.

Chaves, Jamie, and Ashley Taylor. 2021. *The "Why" Behind Classroom Behaviors, Pre-K-5: Integrative Strategies for Learning, Regulation, and Relationships.* Thousand Oaks, CA: Corwin Press.

Chinn, Karen. 1995. *Sam and the Lucky Money.* Illustrated by Cornelius Van Wright and Ying-Hwa Hu. New York: Lee and Low.

Derman-Sparks, Louise, and Julie Olson Edwards. 2020. *Anti-Bias Education for Young Children and Ourselves.* 2nd ed. Washington, DC: NAEYC.

Edwards, Dave. 2025. *Gender Inclusive Schools: How to Affirm and Support Gender-Expansive Students.* Minneapolis, MN: Free Spirit Publishing.

Evans, Betsy. 2016. *You Can't Come to My Birthday! Conflict Resolution with Young Children.* 2nd ed. Ypsilanti, MI: HighScope Press.

Gebauer, Miriam, Nele McElvany, Olaf Köller, and Christian Schöber. 2021. "Cross-Cultural Differences in Academic Self-Efficacy and Its Sources across Socialization Contexts." *Social Psychology of Education* 24:1407–32. https://doi.org/10.1007/s11218-021-09658-3.

Gilliam, Walter S., Angela N. Maupin, Chin R. Reyes, Maria R. Accavitti, and Frederick Shic. 2016. "Do Early Educators' Implicit Biases Regarding Sex and Race Relate to Behavior Expectations and Recommendations of Preschool Expulsions and Suspensions?" Research brief. New Haven, CT: Yale University Child Study Center.

Gray, Peter. 2015. "Studying Play Without Calling It That: Humanistic and Positive Psychology." In *The Handbook of the Study of Play*, vol. 2, edited by James E. Johnson, Scott G. Eberle, Thomas S. Henricks, and David Kuschner, 121–38. Lanham, MD: Rowman and Littlefield.

Han, Jia, Gordon Waddington, Roger Adams, Judith Anson, and Yu Liu. 2016. "Assessing Proprioception: A Critical Review of Methods." *Journal of Sports Health Science* 5 (1): 80–90.

Huber, Mike. 2017. *Embracing Rough-and-Tumble Play: Teaching with the Body in Mind.* St. Paul, MN: Redleaf Press.

———. 2022. *Inclusion Includes Us: Building Bridges and Removing Barriers in Early Childhood Classrooms.* St. Paul, MN: Redleaf Press.

James, Sandy E., Jody L. Herman, Laura E. Durso, and Rodrigo Heng-Lehtinen. 2022. "Early Insights: A Report of the U.S. Transgender Survey." National Center for Transgender Equality. Washington, DC. https://transequality.org/sites/default/files/2024-02/2022%20USTS%20Early%20Insights%20Report_FINAL.pdf. Accessed November 17, 2024.

John Hopkins Bloomberg School of Public Health. 2024. "New Report Highlights U.S. 2022 Gun-Related Deaths: Firearms Remain Leading Cause of Death for Children and Teens, and Disproportionately Affect People of Color." https://publichealth.jhu.edu/2024/guns-remain-leading-cause-of-death-for -children-and-teens.

Jones, Elizabeth, and Renatta M. Cooper. 2006. *Playing to Get Smart*. New York: Teachers College Press.

Katch, Hannah, and Jane Katch. 2010. "When Boys Won't Be Boys: Discussing Gender with Young Children." *Harvard Educational Review* 80 (3): 379–90.

Katch, Jane. 2001. *Under Deadman's Skin: Discovering the Meaning of Children's Violent Play*. Boston: Beacon Press.

King, Donna. 2021. *Pursuing Bad Guys: Joining Children's Quest for Clarity, Courage and Community*. Lincoln, NE: Exchange Press.

Kohn, Alfie. 1993. *Punished by Rewards: The Trouble with Gold Stars, Incentive Plans, A's, and Other Bribes*. Boston: Houghton Mifflin Company.

Kok, Kristiaan P.W., Anne M.C. Loeber, and John Grin. 2021. "Politics of Complexity: Conceptualizing Agency, Power and Powering in the Transitional Dynamics of Complex Adaptive Systems." *Research Policy* 50 (3). https://doi.org/10.1016/j.respol.2020.104183.

Levin, Diane E., and Nancy Carlsson-Paige. 2004. *The War Play Dilemma: What Every Parent and Teacher Needs to Know*. 2nd ed. New York: Teachers College Press.

Li, Ming, Liman Man Wai Li, Ke Zhao, and Ding-Guo Gao. 2019. "Cultural Group Perception Enhances Sense of Agency in a Multicultural Society." *Scandinavian Journal of Psychology* 60 (4): 394–403.

Mayeroff, Milton. 1990. *On Caring*. Reprint edition. New York: Harper Perennial.

Mechling, Jay. 2008. "Gun Play." *American Journal of Play* 1 (2): 192–209.

Merleau-Ponty, Maurice. (1945) 2002. *Phenomenology of Perception*. Translated by Colin Smith. New York: Routledge Classics.

NAEYC (National Association for the Education of Young Children). 2011. "Code of Ethical Conduct and Statement of Commitment." Position statement. Washington, DC: NAEYC. www.naeyc.org/sites/default/files/globally-shared/ downloads/PDFs/resources/position-statements/Ethics%20Position %20Statement2011_09202013update.pdf.

Paley, Vivian Gussin. 1988. *Bad Guys Don't Have Birthdays: Fantasy Play at Four*. Chicago: University of Chicago Press.

Pastel, Encian, Katie Steele, Julie Nicholson, Cyndi Maurer, Julia Hennock, Jonathan Julian, Tess Unger, and Nathanael Flynn. 2019. *Support Gender Diversity in Early Childhood Classrooms: A Practical Guide*. London: Jessica Kingsley Publishers.

Pavlas, Davin. 2010. "A Model of Flow and Play in Game-Based Learning: The Impact of Game Characteristics, Player Traits, and Player States." PhD diss., University of Central Florida. https://stars.library.ucf.edu/etd/1657.

Pearson, Catherine. 2019. "What to Do When Your Son Is Obsessed with Guns." *Huffington Post*, December 2, 2019. www.huffpost.com/entry/son-obsessed-pretend-toy-guns_l_5de52df6e4b0d50f32a62859.

Purves, Dale, George J. Augustine, David Fitzpatrick, Lawrence C. Katz, Anthony-Samuel LaMantia, James O. McNamara, and S. Mark Williams. 2001. "What Is Sex?" In *Neuroscience*. 2nd ed. Sunderland, MA: Sinauer Associates. www.ncbi.nlm.nih.gov/books/NBK10943.

Reyhing, Yvonne, and Sonja Perren. 2021. "Self-Efficacy in Early Childhood Education and Care: What Predicts Patterns of Stability and Change in Educator Self-Efficacy?" *Frontiers in Education* 6: 1–10. https://doi.org/10.3389/feduc.2021.634275.

Rogoff, Barbara. 2015. "It Starts at Home: Letting Children Collaborate." Filmed June 4, 2015, in Santa Cruz, California. TED video, 9:08. www.youtube.com/watch?v=Bu03KUNI1Zk.

Stietz, Julia, Emanuel Jauk, Sören Krach, and Philipp Kanske. 2019 "Dissociating Empathy from Perspective-Taking: Evidence from Intra- and Inter-Individual Differences." *Frontiers in Psychiatry* 10 (March): 126. www.frontiersin.org/journals/psychiatry/articles/10.3389/fpsyt.2019.00126/full.

Theorell, Ebba 2023. *Se krigsleken - kraft rörelse och förvandling*. Stockholm, Sweden: Lärarförlaget.

Trook, Eve. 1983. *Understanding Teachers' Use of Power: A Role-Playing Activity*. TCS Education System, Pacific Oaks College. JSTOR. https://jstor.org/stable/community.31958003.

United Nations. 1989. Convention on the Rights of the Child, Article 31. www.unicef.org/media/52626/file.

The Violence Project. 2021. The Mass Shooter Database. www.theviolenceproject.org/mass-shooter-database.

Vygotsky, Lev S. (1966) 2016. "Play and Its Role in the Mental Development of the Child." Translated by Nikolai Veresov and Myra Barrs. *International Research in Early Childhood Education* 7 (2): 3–25. https://files.eric.ed.gov/fulltext/EJ1138861.pdf.

Wallace, David Foster. 2009. *This Is Water: Some Thoughts Delivered on a Significant Occasion about Living a Compassionate Life*. New York: Little, Brown and Company.

World Federation of Occupational Therapists. 2024. "About Occupational Therapy." https://wfot.org/about/about-occupational-therapy.

Zimmerman, Calvin Rashaud. 2024. "Looking for Trouble: How Teachers' Racialized Practices Perpetuate Discipline Inequities in Early Childhood." *Sociology of Education* 97 (3). https://journals.sagepub.com/doi/10.1177/00380407241228581.

Zola, Ray. 2017. "This Is the Toy Gun That Got Tamir Rice Killed Three Years Ago Today." *Newsweek*, November 22, 2017. www.newsweek.com/tamir-rice-police-brutality-toy-gun-720120.

Index